J. Morlais Jones

The Cup of Cold Water

And Other Sermons

J. Morlais Jones

The Cup of Cold Water
And Other Sermons

ISBN/EAN: 9783744666718

Printed in Europe, USA, Canada, Australia, Japan

Cover: Foto ©Lupo / pixelio.de

More available books at **www.hansebooks.com**

THE
CUP OF COLD WATER

AND OTHER SERMONS

BY THE

REV. J. MORLAIS JONES

LEWISHAM

LONDON
SAMPSON LOW, MARSTON & COMPANY
LIMITED
St. Dunstan's House
FETTER LANE, FLEET STREET, E.C.
1894

LONDON:
PRINTED BY WILLIAM CLOWES AND SONS, LIMITED,
STAMFORD STREET AND CHARING CROSS.

TO

MY BEST FRIEND

AND

BRAVEST HELPER,

MY WIFE.

CONTENTS.

THE CUP OF COLD WATER.

"And whosoever shall give to drink unto one of these little ones a cup of cold water only in the name of a disciple, verily I say unto you, he shall in no wise lose his reward."—MATT. x. 42 1

Preached on Sunday morning, March 26, 1893.

THE LYRIC OF PERFECT TRUST.

"The Lord is my Shepherd; I shall not want. He maketh me to lie down in green pastures: He leadeth me beside the still waters," etc.—Ps. xxiii. 15

THE ONE MASTER.

"One is your Master, even the Christ."—MATT. xxiii. 10 ... 33

Preached on Sunday morning, July 13, 1893.

A GOOD REASON FOR NOT LEAVING CHRIST.

"To whom shall we go?"—JOHN v. 68 49

Preached on Sunday morning, May 28, 1893.

THE BUILDING UP OF CHRISTIAN MANHOOD.

"But ye, beloved, building up yourselves on your most holy faith, praying in the Holy Ghost, keep yourselves in the love of God, looking for the mercy of our Lord Jesus Christ unto eternal life."—JUDE 20, 21 63

Preached as a Heckmondwike Lecture.

AN UNTRAMMELLED LIFE.

"The Lord answered me, and set me in a large place."—Ps. cxviii. 5 85

Preached on Sunday morning, June 4, 1893.

PROPHETS AND SONS OF THE PROPHETS.

"Ye are the sons of the prophets."—ACTS iii. 25 103

Preached on Sunday morning, May 7, 1893.

FAITH FOUND IN UNEXPECTED PLACES.

"Verily I say unto you, I have not found so great faith, no, not in Israel."—MATT. viii. 10 119

Preached on Sunday morning, January 8, 1893.

THE FATHERHOOD OF GOD.

"Our Father."—MATT. vi. 9 137

Preached on Sunday morning, October 1, 1893.

OUR SALVATION INTELLIGIBLE IN THE LIGHT OF GOD'S LOVE.

"God is love."—1 JOHN iv. 8 155

Preached on Sunday morning, December 4, 1892.

READING.

"Till I come, give attendance to reading."—1 TIM. iv. 13 ... 167

Preached on Sunday evening, March 12, 1893.

BLITHE CHILDHOOD AND BLITHER OLD AGE.

"Thou makest the outgoings of the morning and evening to rejoice."—Ps. lxv. 8 185

Preached on Sunday morning, April 9, 1893.

CONSIDERATENESS.

"Let your considerateness be known unto all men."—PHIL. iv. 5 201

Preached on Sunday morning, November 13, 1892.

CUP OF COLD WATER.

THE CUP OF COLD WATER.

"And whosoever shall give to drink unto one of these little ones a cup of cold water only in the name of a disciple, verily I say unto you, he shall in no wise lose his reward."—MATT. x. 42.

I. LIFE'S REAL WEALTH CONSISTS OF LITTLE THINGS. "A cup of cold water." We are *beginning* to believe in cold water, to understand its virtues, to see what a miracle-worker it is. Two of the great words of the Bible are "bread" and "water"—the two things we cannot live without; always the symbols which Jesus used to typify the preciousness of His gospel—the one absolute necessity, without which life was haggard, poor, impossible. "I am the Bread of life;" "If thou knewest the gift of God, . . . thou wouldest have asked of Him, and He would have given thee living water." In the vision John sees of a perfect world, the gospel flows through it as "the river of the water of life."

We will pause there at the very beginning. Life's absolute necessities—bread, water,—every one has *them*. And the gospel—the "well of water" into which every one of us may dip his cup—that is barriered against nobody. Oh, we may live a brave, wise, grand life ; see the best, taste the best, know the best. Let us vow to ourselves that henceforth we do not mean to moan.

And now let us look at this for a little while.

1. Life's most perfect gifts, life's most perfect mercies, are *little* things. "A cup of cold water." We have somehow become singularly blind and demented. We set before ourselves as life's most perfect prizes, the summing up of life, the essence of its bliss, the things which the experience of every age has proved have no relation to *genuine* bliss at all. We strive and deny ourselves, become untrue to our divinest longings, strangle our noblest instincts in order to possess them, and they leave us hungry and haggard as ever. Marvellous how the dream of *wealth* fascinates men. Gold has only to show itself, and we will pursue it over the souls of our children, trample upon the love of those who will crush their life out to refresh ours, and sponge every reminiscence of God out of our souls for its sake. And yet, what can it do? It cannot set one line of nobleness in a man's face. Ugly, demon gold! *Learning*, I acknowledge, has many charms, but it has also its special miseries. The glass-worker who keeps constantly peering into the white heat gradually becomes blind; and the scholar, the philosopher, the so-called leader of thought, sometimes keeps peering so incessantly into the light that he ceases to see. I have read Kant and Hegel; I have read Professor Green, the English expounder of Hegel. Every one of them seems to have looked so long into the light that he has become half-blind. The story of *genius* has been a sad one. Misery has so persistently been its shadow, that one is more than half ready to believe that genius is only another name for insanity, and to pray over one's children that whatever misfortune may lie before them, they may be saved at least from every taint of that.

We laugh at these ambitions when they appear as small vanities. We ridicule the man who tortures his soul and makes himself miserable in the name of what he calls art; who has not a chair in his drawing-room upon which he dares *sit;* to whom the sofa upon which he might fling himself and *rest* would be an æsthetic horror. We laugh at him. But the man who groans under the weight of what every one supposes to be life's most perfect prizes— genius, learning, wealth—we will not laugh at, we will pity him. I offer you my sympathy, any of you who may be fretting under the fever of your great gifts, or drinking from the fountain of your great success, and wondering how it is that you are not happy. You drink, but somehow that water has no power to quench your thirst. Dear friends, listen. It is common things, simple things, that quench thirst; not spiced wine, but the "cup of cold water." Health, work, genuine friendship, the caresses of little children, the love that set its hand in yours one beautiful morning five and twenty years ago, which has become deeper, richer, sweeter, as your head has grown grey. God's sweet, simple gifts! A soul which is always young, which is as fresh in old age as when it came first from the hand of God. That is life's most precious wealth, life's most perfect gift. The "cup of cold water."

2. The most real help that we can render one another lies in things that cost very little. You may not be able to do much, but you can give to somebody who needs it "a cup of cold water."

The fact is, we can do much for one another, and we can do nothing. Wait there for a moment. You cannot do my work, and I do not ask you to do it. I received it, a sealed secret from the hand of God, and no one can open it but myself. I must be often alone with it—wrestle with it, as Jacob did through dark and weary hours, whilst others are sleeping peacefully enough. You cannot fight my battles. I must strangle my own doubts, face the spectres and ghosts for myself. Nobody knows where the iron enters my soul. I must face my own sins, choke the temptations that are throttling me with my own hand. I must enter the chamber of sorrows, and, like Abraham, bow before my dead alone. And the end will come, and no one can come with me. Like Hiawatha, I must release myself from every tie; I must step into the boat alone; go out and "cross the bar," go down into the light of sunset, disappear in the shadow of evening—*alone*. Life is intensely, absolutely personal. I can be excused nothing, and I am proud of it. I shall some day go back to God, and carry with me this "Book of Life"—the record of what I have thought, said, done, been; from "Title-page" to "Finis," every word written in it will be mine. The awfulness, but grandeur and sublimity of life! Dear friends, you can do nothing for me.

But, oh yes, you can. You can excuse me no duty, you cannot save me from one yard of the road; but when I am fagged, disheartened, and weary, you can give me "a cup of cold water." I have seen a picture of the soldiers passing through a village on their way to the front. It has been a long march, and every one is weary and footsore. There has been hard fighting, but there is more fighting still to be in front. The villagers crowd around them, pressing food and refreshment upon them. The villagers cannot save them from the battle, but they can cheer them as they go; and everything the village holds in the shape of food and help is thrust upon them. And so here. We *must* go to the battle; no one can save me from that. There are duties from which no one can excuse me; disciplines, sorrows, struggles come in the common lot of all. But oh, I know how to equip myself. I have books which are storehouses of noble thought, and I shut myself up for an hour's reading, and rise from the reading like a giant refreshed. I have friends whose words are an inspiration; whose strong faith, whose brave counsel, brings summer into my soul; whom no winter can withstand. I am a man of many moods, of many despairs; but the light in the faces of some whom I know, the grasp of their hand, their genius to comfort, is irresistible. I can dare anything, I fear nothing; all fears vanish when they speak. They have given me "a cup of cold water."

3. Once again: Our real salvation, the things which refresh and put heart into us, are the *simplicities* of the gospel—the "cup of cold water."

Geology is a grand science; get an enthusiast to expound it, and you begin to feel that everything depends upon geology. Volcanoes used to be the symbol of everything terrible to me when I was a boy. But I have read Charles Kingsley. Charles Kingsley was a scientist, but he was a poet also in every fibre of his soul; and it is only a scientist who is a poet that can expound his own science. Charles Kingsley showed how the great volcanoes have been God's most glorious workers. Every harvest in the fruitful plains of Europe is due to the beneficent work of the volcanoes ages ago; every grain of the rich soil was melted out of the solid granite. It is a romantic story, a perfect fairy tale, an enchantment, if you know how to read it, if you have the imagination to picture the whole process to yourself. But the embarrassed farmer with a hundred calls upon him, who finds it hard work to provide for his children, has little heart to think of those things; he only wonders what the next harvest is going to be. You can listen to Wagner's music now and then. You pull your soul together and half blush that you do not find the romantic depths in it that its enthusiatic expounder wants you to see; you hush your soul to listen; you rebuke yourself that you are not more interested; and you secretly wonder what the enchantment is which others find in it. But, in your fagged and weary moments, "Home, Sweet Home" means more to you than every note that Wagner ever composed. So, the great mysteries of theology: oh, they *ought* to be studied—I am always contending for that—and we pull ourselves together and resolutely set ourselves to the study now and then. The Trinity; the Atonement; the fundamental question of God,—the existence of God; the great laws in the light of which we must determine the awful problem of our final destiny: oh, we must dissolve them now and then in the crucible of our hardest and keenest thinking. Depend upon it, that to give up thinking is to impoverish the gospel. But those matters are not our real salvation. There come times when those things are not bread, but stones—a highly flavoured and elaborately cooked feast, but we cannot eat it. You have laid out the table grandly. Like Ahasuerus at his banquet, you have set out "vessels of gold" and poured "royal wine" into them; but I am thirsty, and the fever is in my blood still; I crave for "a cup of cold water." "God is love;" "God so loved the world, that He gave His only begotten Son;" "Believe on the Lord Jesus Christ, and thou shalt be saved;" "Him that cometh unto Me I will in no wise cast out;" "Christ Jesus came into the world to save sinners;" "Where *I* am, there shall *ye* be also;" "I go to prepare a place for you." *That* is the "cup of cold water:" I drink deep of it; it quenches my thirst; I am young again; despair is gone; I am master of life; nothing can quail me. Ay, it is the "cup of cold water" that we need.

II. IN THE LIGHT OF THAT WE CAN ALL OF US RENDER REAL SERVICE. We may not, perhaps, be able to do much; but we can all of us give some weak one, some fainting, insignificant one, "a cup of cold water." Heal the sick we cannot; physicians we are not; but we can bend over the fever-stricken one, in whose veins the fire is burning, and set to his parched lips the "cup of cold water." Let me say there—

1. First: Great things the majority of us cannot do. The great mountains that determine the climate of Europe are very few; there is only one range of Alps. Great writers seldom come. Tennyson is dead, and England is beginning to wonder whether she shall ever have another poet. The great books that create an era are few and far between. Many a man has imagined himself to be a Shakespeare; but England says, "No, there has never been but one." Scientists are plentiful as blackberries, and a noisy brood they are; but the Bacons, the Newtons, the Darwins, appear at rare, rare intervals. "Great is the company of the preachers;" but the Spurgeons and Henry Ward Beechers are very few, and the great theologians are fewer still. You can get six times six hundred and seventy members every time you want to elect a "House of Commons," if you like; but there are not six *statesmen* in the House of Commons at the present moment. Talkers, quibblers, hobby-riders, obstructionists in a multitude (why, even *I* could be an obstructionist); but the Pitts, the Dis-

raelis, and—we shall believe it by-and-by—the Gladstones can easily be counted. Clergymen, ministers, enthusiastic and devoted men, the Church never lacks; the East End, and all the dreariest regions of London, are crowded with them. But there is only one Samuel Barnett—God bless him! He looked, the last time I saw him, as if a breath might have blown him away; but he is the genius, the good angel of Whitechapel. Great souls, rare souls, whom God has hewn after a large mould—we must leave the world's supreme tasks to them. To look at these tasks paralyzes us, and we dare not attempt them. But we can all of us do little things. You have mourned when you have felt the stir of God's Spirit in you; there was nothing which you could do; you were poor, you were not a man of many gifts, there was not one line of genius in you; but there are a hundred *little* things in this place which you can do, and which are crying to be done. A Church may get into inextricable confusion because the little things are neglected. There are sick people whom you can visit, and for this God has endowed some of you with the special gift. Some of you were foreordained to be "sons of consolation," and I *know* it. You came to me when my life seemed to be ebbing out and my heart was breaking, and you did more for me than an archbishop could have done. My soul was half-delirious with fever, but you put the "cup of cold water" to my lips, and I knew the joy and thrill of life again. God bless you, who helped me to believe in heaven, when the darkness of the pit seemed to be shutting in upon me; who saved me from despair, and reset me in the ecstasy of faith, when the last light of absolute truth seemed to be going out.

2. The greatest thing is poor if the little thing be not

done. The miserablest homes I have ever known have often been those that ought to have been the happiest; I envied them before I got to know the whole story. The house was a palace; the head of the household had worked hard, had made money; he could command every luxury, and it was his one pride that everything that money could command was at the disposal of every member of his home-circle; art had done its best, culture had added its sweetest ministries; everything there—everything but the delicate courtesies, the ingenious devices of love, which are life's most perfect graces. Poor Mrs. Carlyle—hers is one of the most pathetic stories of the century to me—a brilliant soul, fit mate for any man however gifted; she had commanded everything she had bidden for—fame, renown, *éclat*—but her heart was starved. She pined for the love that would have been like the dew to her soul. She had married a man of genius, but she had married a savage. One of the great religious newspapers has been dinning for weeks with the complaints of those who consider themselves ignored in our congregations. The cry has been an exceeding "bitter cry"—in many senses utterly unreasonable; selfish souls always expect too much. But the cry is in some respects a just one; on the lips of many it is not a mere complaint, but a wail—the cry of the lonely and neglected. It *is* hard that a man should come to our churches month after month and that no one should pay him any of the small courtesies of civilized life. You pretend to come here to worship God and to study the Lord Jesus, and you never even say "Good morning" to the man who—you have only to look at him and you see it—is a stranger, and who longs more for somebody's "Good morning" than for any brilliant thing that may come from the pulpit. We are for ever talking of the power of the pulpit to win men ; we are constantly insisting that the one weak feature of our churches is the pulpit; that the great need of the hour is an efficient pulpit; a strong, well-read, many-sided pulpit—the lithe brain, the keen eye, the silver tongue, in the pulpit. If the pulpit were up to the mark, our churches would never be empty. Ay, ay! pelt the pulpit; any one can fling a clod out of the crowd at the man in the pulpit. But you may do that without rendering any very signal service to anybody. I am not going to stand up for the pulpit; I will only say that the pulpit in most of the churches which I know does its duty, so that it need make no apology to the pew. What people miss is not brilliancy in the pulpit; it is what *you* can give—the "cup of cold water"— the little things which can never be done by the man who stands here; which must be done by the people who sit there.

III. AND NOW: THE SMALLEST, SIMPLEST MINISTRIES RECEIVE THE FULLEST RECOGNITION OF OUR LORD. "Verily I say unto you, he shall in no wise lose his reward."

1. Our Lord sees how great the smallest ministry is ; how the little thing may show how great the heart is out of which it issues. It is small men neglect the minor courtesies, which do so much to oil the wheels, to soften the jars, and to heal the heartaches of the world. You take a flower into the sick-room, and the sufferer makes a perfect Shechinah of it. He sees the hand of summer and inhales the breath of the garden in it. God has touched it into beauty—nay, God has looked upon it, and it has blushed into beauty. It is an altar, and your love burns upon it, and sweet is the incense of it to the weary one. You talk of "the language of flowers ;" why, *that* is "the language of flowers"—the

chant which the flower goes on singing by that sick-bed. Great are little things; and Christ reads everything; He misses nothing of the meaning of the smallest act. Christ is the supreme Poet, and the "cup of cold water" is a divine lyric to Him.

I have seen the glass indicator set in the front of the steam-boiler; a small tube three inches long or so. It told me exactly what force of steam was working in that boiler; I knew exactly what power of work was hidden there. Or I will use another illustration. The other morning I saw an ingenious machine which told with the minutest exactitude the strength of a bar of metal put to the test. You had only to look at the indicator, and it told you within the hundredth fraction of a pound what weight that bar of metal could bear. So the smallest thing may indicate the force of Christian life, the store of Christian self-denial, the power of Christian service, there is in you. The prayer-meeting—every one just now pooh-poohs the prayer-meeting, but it may be an indicator of how much the Christian life means to you. The weekly offering means nothing, so you think, but a perverse device for worrying men who want to forget money at least once a week; but it may be the mark upon the indicator which shows how dear the house of God is to you. It is the "cup of cold water," an index of what your heart is.

And now, lastly—

2. The Lord's reward to you will be, not according to the measure of the "cup of cold water," but of what the "cup of cold water" indicated. Wonderful is the story of the judgment as told by Jesus. Amazement fills those whom He sets on His right hand. "When saw we Thee a-hungered, or athirst, or sick, and in prison, and ministered

unto Thee?" And He answers, "Inasmuch as ye did it unto one of these little ones"—in these little things—"ye did it unto Me." You have sorrowed and moaned over yourself. You have envied the missionary; the grandeur and pathos of his story have thrilled you; you have looked at the small sphere in which you have worked; you have hung down your head as you have thought of your Sunday school class; you have been ashamed of the petty service you have rendered. Ah, *this* will be your life as Christ will sum it up; as *He* reads it, you also will have been a missionary. You have merely been a watcher over your father's sick-bed—a prisoner. You have envied those whose hands were free—*your* hands have been always tied; you have no record in the Church. Listen! This will be the summing up of it—"Ye did it unto Me;" and the wonder of that will fill you for ever.

THE LYRIC OF PERFECT TRUST.

THE LYRIC OF PERFECT TRUST.

" The Lord is my Shepherd; I shall not want. He maketh me to lie down in green pastures: He leadeth me beside the still waters," etc.
—Ps. xxiii.

"THE nightingale of Psalms," somebody called that—filling the night, flooding it with its song when every other song is hushed. "'The pearl of Psalms," another has called it—pure, beautiful, and beyond price. "The Pleiades," says a third, among the constellations into which these ancient singers have mapped the heaven of love and hope and peace which bent over them.

The comparisons are true and appropriate, and there are some of you who could add other comparisons quite as true and quite as appropriate. You could remember this when you could remember nothing else. In the sickness, when the brain was too weary to think, it came unbidden. In the sorrow which stunned you, you had the sense of a beneficent presence; it penetrated through your stupor and found you, and though you could not argue, you knew that all was well with you. In the presence of dim, undefined fears, when the management of your life had passed out of your hands, when you had neither the skill, the courage, nor the strength to manage it, it hovered about you, and you had the conviction that no harm could befall you. Nightingale, pearl, brightest among all the bright constellations, in which God has written His love and care across the heavens, which encompass the earth and every destiny which is being worked out upon the face of it.

But now, I must not spend the morning in quoting or coining general panegyrics upon this sweet lyric cry. I have a definite idea in my mind—only one—which I wish to place before you. Here is a man who believed in God—believed in Him in no fictitious sense. God was not a mere idea to him—a philosophic abstraction; not a name to cover what has been called "the sum-total of existence," but a living Being with whom he had entered into living relations; whom he believed in, trusted, loved; in whose hands his destiny was, and upon whose goodness and care the issues of his life depended more than upon himself.

It has been discovered in these days—the discovery has been made, I believe, in some peculiarity in the genius of the Hebrew language—that the Jew—and this man was a Jew—did not attribute personality to his God. The great idea the Jew had always before his mind—and it was only an idea—was righteousness. All the currents of the universe set towards that, converged upon that. Everything "made for" righteousness, in the long run *told* for righteousness. But it never entered into his head that there was a *mind*— a hand which determined the course of the currents. God there was not, who thought, willed, ruled. The universe itself was God—omnipotent, righteous, but blind, and impersonal. Now, we are beginning to get tired of all this; there is really no arguing the matter with one who talks thus. If a person will persist in saying that David did not mean a "Person" when he said, "The Lord is my Shepherd," all you can say is, "We had better change the subject and talk about something else." You will let me say, then—what am I talking about? you believe it as firmly as I do—David had in his mind a Personal Being of infinite love, wisdom, and beneficence, whom he had made *his own*—"my Shepherd"—under whose eye, under whose protection, he was living out his little day. And now, what has such a man to say of life? How does it look to him? What is the verdict which he passes upon it?

Four things strike us in his view of life.

I. FIRST: THE WEALTH, COMPLETENESS, FULNESS OF IT. It is something worth possessing. "He maketh me to lie down in green pastures . . . Thou preparest a table before me . . . my cup runneth over."

A new science has been developed of late—the science of being miserable. Men have always been miserable, but it has been reserved for this century to reduce the world's misery into a science. The edifying spectacle has been seen on the continent of Europe, of a supremely able man, who possessed in a rare degree the gift of fascinating others; and he has a sufficient number of followers in England to form what is called a "school," with its expounders and poets. He was well educated, rich, had enjoyed every advantage which the universities of Germany could render him; he had never from childhood had a moment's anxiety as to the wherewithal of life; had never been obliged to do a stroke of work to procure for himself a meal. And in the midst of this easy, well-furnished life—for he never stinted himself in anything—he deliberately proposed to himself to collect every fact which would go to prove how miserable was the lot of man, what a wretched inheritance life was. And he did it. Ransacked every sphere of life, classified his evidence, and gave to the world as his verdict—the summing up of life—"Life is a misfortune, and none but the dead are happy." And there has never been a man classified amongst philosophers who has been more lauded, even abjectly admired, lifted so completely into the position of a demigod. It would not be worth while mentioning this, were it not that his exposition of life is accepted by a good many who have won the ear of the public in England just now. These men possess the literary gift, possess the art of "putting" things—putting even the science of misery in a fascinating form, and investing it with the glamour of sentiment which many mistake for poetry. You cannot open a newspaper or a magazine but you come across some monody in prose or poetry of exquisite sadness. Every drawing-room table holds some delicately bound volume—melancholy has even got to be one of the fine arts—in which you have, on the most artistic paper, some "study" of misery, some diluted doctrine of Schopenhauer.

Then, side by side with this, is a mistaken and exaggerated—I will not say *piety*, but *pietism*—which, in the name of religion, takes hold of everything by the wrong end; which is always sighing—very unreal sighs, though—over our present lot as "a waste, howling wilderness;" always warning those who are getting ready to go out into life. Here they are, brimming over with expectation; the white years, inexhaustible in their resources, lie before them; they look out into the future with infinite hopes, impatient to realize it, for it is all a wonder and a strong desire to them. But, forsooth, it is our duty to warn them to expect no real satisfaction there. The years which promise so much, and which look so beautiful, at best bear but a scant harvest. Better be prepared for disappointment, for weariness, for pains and heartaches, for the perishing of hopes, for diligent sowing to be followed by no happy harvests, for "vanity of vanities." Now, that is pessimism too, and on the whole, I believe, more wicked than the other. Better blast the world in any name than in the name of religion.

Just look. Things *are* what you *make them* be. Life is what you make it. I had occasion to go the other day into a region of London with which I am not very familiar, and I thought I had never seen such a desolate region before. Covered with the poorest specimens of the builder's art, which the inhabitants evidently did not consider worth while looking after. Nothing was done to modify or soften their ungainliness. It did look a hopeless enterprise, I will acknowledge; it *was* an absolute wilderness—the reign of dust and ugliness was complete. But in the midst of the wretched dilapidation was *one* house—*was* it the same as the rest? Could it be the same? The same. In the long terrace the same as all the rest, but transformed into something so beautiful that it made the rest more hideous still. Delicate creepers hung about the steps and climbed up into the windows. Flowers which would have been at home in a Kentish hedgerow kept smiling company in the few yards of space within the railings. Ferns, so fresh that they might have escaped that morning from a Devonshire lane, grew out of all manner of impossible corners. "The desert shall blossom like the rose," I said. There it was, and my heart blessed those within, whoever they were, who had saved that neighbourhood from contempt. That is a parable. That is life: according to what you put into it, according to what you make it or allow it to become—" a waste, howling wilderness," or the garden of God. You may write a "Book of Lamentations" over it, or a "Twenty-third Psalm;" say, "there is nothing in life worth living for, nothing worth possessing;" or, "He maketh me to lie down in green pastures: He leadeth me beside the still waters ... Thou preparest a table before me ... Thou anointest my head with oil; *my cup runneth over.*"

Now, will you look at this for a moment or two in detail? Of course I am speaking right through of the man who has a personal hold of God; I am not speaking of life in the abstract, of life in *any* case, of what *is* apart from every condition, but of what is when the man can say, "God is mine."

And the first thought, as I have said, is the wealth, completeness, fulness of life. See how it is put. *Full provision is made for all the necessities of man's nature.* Life is *a feast:* "Thou preparest a table for me." Now, do not limit that to the mere supplying of man's physical necessities; that is to have a very imperfect perception of the meaning of the words. "Thou preparest a table" for every side of my nature; life is a feast all round; Thou satisfiest whatever in me hungers.

Now we will see. Is our life so poor as we say it is, when we fall into conventional ways of talking? Is the cup of life so empty that it only mocks the man who tries to quench his thirst by it?

I will tell you how life looks to me.

First, I AM—personal existence is mine. I have a being, the integrity, the sanctity of which even God respects, the boundaries of which even my Maker does not trench upon. One of Miss Martineau's friends—and he not a fool—once turned upon her, when she was complacently consigning herself and everybody else to death and nothingness, and thundered, "I had rather be damned than annihilated." "Amen," say I. The thrill of realizing one's personal existence is sometimes overpowering. All honours and privileges which can come to me from the hands of my Maker can only be second to this—He has considered me worthy *to be*. Among the worthy ideas, the imperishable facts of the universe, that embodied in my existence has been considered by Him—and His judgment is the measure of worth—worthy also. The universe as *He* saw it, the great thought which He is working out, and which the ages only will unfold, would not have been complete without ME. Reverence yourself. There is a bit of God in *you*, in every one which He has reproduced or repeated nowhere else.

Then, *the world is mine*. The heavens and the earth are mine. I have seen a bit of colour on a cloud which half made me a believer in ancient mythology—in the gods flashing their robes for a moment into visibility; sunsets that were worth being born to see; sunrises as glorious as that which ordained Wordsworth to the vocation of a poet. A banquet has been spread before me on a summer's afternoon on the side of a Welsh hill upon which I have feasted for a twelvemonth.

Then, *there is the world of ideas*, which come greeting you like troops of angels; from the books of gifted souls; from the mystic recesses of your own heart, bearing the mark upon their brow—"We are the children of God, emanations from the wisdom in Him; you can safely receive us and make us your lifelong guests."

Then, *friendship has been yours*. Love, the wine of life. The clasp of the tiny arms, the laughter and sweet trust of little children, which cast out devils. The joy of serving, the joy of charity, the joy of dispensing sympathy, of bearing burdens which are not your own; the benediction of those to whom you have been a good Samaritan. You have had "Thank you" said to you as you left the sick-room, or lifted some anxiety out of some one's lot, in a way which made you repeat it to yourself all the way home. It was music to you; it made your feet dance.

The happiness and ennoblement of benefiting the world— that is yours. Three young men in England and three in Germany—the group there knowing nothing of the group here, Bunsen being the leader there, and John Herschell here—entered into a solemn covenant with one another that they *would* leave the world better than they found it. *You* may put yourself into that covenant, if you please; and the harvest you will reap in your own soul will be a hundredfold for the seed you sow. Life poor? Its joys scant? We may manage to scrape together, contrive or steal what may keep the soul from starving? Nay! Full measure, pressed down, is given us if we will: our "cup *runneth over.*"

II. LOOK SECONDLY. HERE IS THE SENSE OF PERFECT SECURITY, OF ABSOLUTE FREEDOM FROM ALL ANXIETY. "Goodness and mercy shall follow me all the days of my life."

What a load would be lifted off some minds in this congregation if they could only say that, and be sure of it— "Goodness and mercy shall follow me all the days of my life!" I know people—not a few—to whom I could say, "You are spoiling your life through the dread of what *may be* somewhere in the future; your health is being undermined, you are becoming nervous and depressed." I look at their work and might say, "This is not the kind of work *you* ought to produce—there is no relation between this and your gifts; but what can a man do with an agitated brain and a trembling hand?" I ask, "Have the years vanquished you?" "Oh no; they have dealt kindly with me. Difficulties *did* appear, but I faced them and they vanished; the road did often seem as if it were coming to an end, but it always opened out and there was a further prospect beyond; deep rivers have crossed my path, but at the touch of my foot they divided, and I passed over on dry land." "*The present, then?* Does *it* hem you in? Do you sit down to a bare, unprovided table?" "No." "Is the meal in the barrel exhausted; has the cruse of oil run dry?" "No, but——" "But what?" "But I can feel that it is all *but* exhausted, and the cruse of oil must be running low. Thank God, I have been equal to my work in the past—I have never been beaten yet; but the future, the future!"

Listen to me. The people of Israel, whose pilgrimage of forty years was a parable of life, were spending their first day in the desert. The sweet waters of the Nile were far away—they had left the last well behind them. Darkness came down upon a people filled with dread; anxiety sealed their eyelids that night. But when the morning broke there was the sound of running water in the camp. Ah, if that could *last!* But the desert was before them, and they drank with sad foreboding; this bountiful stream would soon be dried. But the months, the years passed, and that camp was never pitched beyond the sound of water. So, in the home where you first began to realize that the world had to be managed, that the wherewithal did not come without toil, your little life was already pitched within sound of the river of God. There were conferences often, which you did not understand, between the father and mother who are long since gone, whose grave is the sacredest spot on earth to you. There was a sad look in their faces which was a mystery to you, but you were never out of the sound of the river. The day to step over the threshold came. I could put you within six inches of the spot on the road where my mother and I parted nearly forty years ago. Your path has been a devious one since then; you have passed through many experiences, the landscape of your life has often changed; you have built a home of your own since then—*on the banks of the river*—and your children know the voice of it now. And here you are, scaring yourself with imaginary possibilities; you are drying up the river which has flowed with you thus far, and conjuring a desert where its voice will be no longer heard. Faithless man! Ay, faithless man, who says that he believes in God out of whose hand the river flows. *Can* you so misconstrue the years? The last sound that shall reach you, the last voice, when the voices of love and friendship shall be hushed in death, will be *the river—the river*. Goodness and mercy shall follow you all the days of your life—and *beyond*.

III. BUT AGAIN: YOU HAVE THE RECORD HERE OF DELIVERANCES, RESTORATIONS. "He restoreth my soul." You must not make a mistake; the Psalm does not give an altogether rose-coloured view of life. The first part of this sermon may have only irritated you. "That may be all very pleasant," you have said; "but that is not life—at least, it is not *my* life. Life is full of perils, full of pains, haunted by dark fears." My dear friend, all that is understood here. The perils, the fears, are *implied*, if not plainly stated. They are the background of the Psalm, but that only brings out the Psalm into brighter relief. It is the cry of confidence, the song of security which has been learnt in the midst of perils; it is inspired by the memory of signal deliverances, it is confidence gained by witnessing what God can do.

I remember one spot in Switzerland which made a most lasting impression upon me. I heard there the most exquisite music it had ever been my lot to hear. I had never known the power of music before, never understood what a magician man could be. It was at Freibourg. The man sat at his wonderful organ, and called voices at his bidding from the divine heights and from the mystic deeps. There was a thunderstorm among the mountains. We could hear it march every moment nearer, until it culminated in a crash which made the cathedral in which we sat tremble. But across the storm we could hear a hymn—the sweet voices of women, and the sweeter voices of little children, clear, liquid, triumphant, until at last the storm died away into a peace like heaven; but the sweet voices still sang on. Now, that is this Psalm. The *thunder* is here; the "blackness of darkness," the enemy, the scares, the fears, are here. But above everything the voice of *faith* is here; confident, victorious, thrilling with memories of unexpected restorations—deliverances which only a divine hand could have effected. Look at it for a moment.

1. Take the dark side first. Here it is in a sentence: "Yea, though I walk through the valley of the shadow of death." That is not the valley of *death*. John Bunyan understood that well enough, as you remember. You follow his "Pilgrim" and "the valley of the shadow of death" comes long before the end.

I will tell you what it is. The *valley of doubt*. That is "the valley of the shadow of death;" and the shadow of death *does* fall across it. Belief is dead in you; there is certainty nowhere. Everything turns upon you in the shape of a denial, presents itself to you as a note of interrogation; and behind that is a sneer. Ironical laughter fills your soul; the sweet story of Jesus has lost its charm; virtue and holiness have no existence. Go where you will, read what you will, and Mephistopheles looks over your shoulder, and his "Ha, ha!" at your attempts to believe turns your blood cold. *That* is "the valley of the shadow of death."

Sorrow into which you can put no meaning. The life which has been most completely blessed, where love in its noblest forms has been ministering, finds itself suddenly deserted; the heart distracted and tortured with purposeless agonies, ploughed into furrows into which no merciful hand drops the seed which may grow up hereafter into a harvest of joy and sustenance. You, my poor brother, you are in "the valley of the shadow of death."

The agony of remorse. Consternation at a devastated and misspent life. I am not speaking of repentance; repentance has not come yet. That will lift the shadow; but it is only shame and horror as yet. The ruined years are beginning to turn upon you; the past rises like a ghost from its grave and confronts you, and—horror of horrors!—*that* is my life! *You* are in "the valley of the shadow of death."

2. But now, even from these things does God restore us. Very graphic is this language; nothing could more impressively say how absolutely deliverance from these things comes from God. "He *restoreth* my soul." Engulfed, overwhelmed in these things, He giveth back my soul to me. And that is just it. I will retrace my steps.

Shall I speak of forgiveness? It is to give back my soul to me. I remember it well. I remember when all my delusions were swept away, and I saw at last what I had been making of myself, what I was getting to be. My eyes were opened. I walked in great dread; I was cursed. My life—glorious in its possibilities—wasted, impoverished, ruined. God was at one end of the universe and I at the other, and between us was the vast void. No light came across, no tender voice, no message of love. *There*, the great, the infinite, the blessed God; *here*, miserable me. But He stretched His hand across the infinite separation; He lifted me over. It was incipient heaven. Perhaps you make little of this forgiveness to-day. Oh, you will want it some day—cry for it, hunger and thirst for it! You will want the ugly wrong buried; you will want the white-winged angels of the merciful to take it up and bear it swiftly away, where all is forgotten. Forgiveness! Forgiveness! When it came, it was sunrise, it was summer; it was a great joy that *possessed* you. It was finding life again; it was giving you your soul back again. "He restoreth my soul."

Or sorrow. You have known that. The thunderbolt suddenly descended from a clear sky, and left your happy home a desolation. You made a vow to yourself that you would never sit down to the feast of life again; it would be faithlessness to the dead to find pleasure in life any more. You have not *argued* yourself back; certainly you have not forgotten. Forgotten! You can never forget. But one by one has He given back the interests of life to you. He has *restored* your life to you, and you live again, and that without treason to those who are gone.

Or doubt. I have watched many through that episode. I have seen the first signs of the unrest and dissatisfaction which told me that the fever was coming. I have been with them in the wild delirium, when their old beliefs lay in shattered fragments at their feet. And I have seen them again emerge into health and a happy faith. But I have never seen one restored by reading, by research, by the mere help of well-put arguments; simply convinced and lifted back again into life by the intellect. Forgive me if I give you a piece of personal experience. I remember a time when my faith had vanished from me. I had read myself into a fog; committed myself to the guidance of authors who had proved Judas Iscariots to me, who betrayed me with a kiss. A haze and bewilderment hung over the pages of the New Testament; and in my misery I had still to preach, when I was sure of nothing, when I could not put out my hand and say with absolute confidence, "*This* and *this* is truth." But I determined I would read no more. I would take the Gospel of St. John, and keep myself to that. And I did. I opened no other book for months. I saturated my soul with St. John, got it into my blood and bones. And listen! it healed me; my faith came back again to me; my soul was *restored* to me. Oh, young people, I can speak no word of condemnation to you; but you read, read, read, and the more you read, the more perplexed, the more bewildered, you get! Give over reading for a while; go home and lock up the books for a season. Give *God* a chance; hand yourselves over to Him, and see if He will not restore your soul to you.

IV. And now, lastly, here is a determination arising from this experience of God. "I will dwell in the house of the Lord for ever."

That does not mean, of course, merely the material

house; it means much more. It means—I will live in free intercourse, in frank fellowship, in unbroken friendship, with God. That, if you like, is the first meaning. But it does mean the material house also—the temple of the Lord, where we meet to renew our vows, and to remind ourselves in concert of the God who is the Inspiration of our life. My sermon would be incomplete if I did not emphasize the help which this may be to you; the beneficent power it may be in your religious life; the worth of the companionships, the friendships, the worship, the tender associations which, as the years move on, gather around it —how they root the soul in the things which are its real salvation.

I have no words in which I can express to you what I feel on this matter—what a home in the house of the Lord may be to you. I have been a village minister; I know the anxiety of fathers, and especially of mothers, when the boy goes from home for the first time. They have come to me and said, "If I could only find a home for the boy in some Christian family, that would relieve my anxiety." Ah, it *is* a terrible thing to be in London without a home! I could tell you tales that would wring your hearts—tragic stories of the brightest and bravest lives that have ended in disaster; and one word would explain it all—homeless in London, homeless on the sabbath.

Hear me. One home you can have—"the house of the Lord." I do not want to rave and cant, but I knew a minister whom I begged to commend his boys — and brilliant boys they were—to some Christian Church when they left him. Oh, that did not matter; there was no peril for such boys as his. They would be with friends, here, there, everywhere, on the Sunday; they would hear all manner of preaching—he wished them to hear it; it would be good for them. He said to me before he died, "I wish I had listened to you." They were Christian youths when they came up to our fascinating, perilous, bewildering city; but they have every one of them made shipwreck of the faith. Oh, have a home—have a sabbath home! In any case, say this to-day, "I will make my home near God, near His commandments, near His precepts, near His counsel, near His love." Do this, and no harm shall befall you. "I will dwell in the house of the Lord for ever."

THE ONE MASTER.

D—20

THE ONE MASTER.

"One is your Master, even the Christ."—MATT. xxiii. 10.

MAN has only one Master in religion. You may be my master in a thousand other matters; my master in literature, in science, in intellectual gifts and training. I respect and do homage to you; I wonder at your feats; I see you do with consummate ease what is a toil and trouble to me. You climb the mountain heights, you cross gorge and glacier, you are perfectly at home where I do not even dare try to stand. I watch you, fascinated, but I dare not try to do what you do. In those things I willingly acknowledge you to be my master. There are authorities in history, in science, in scholarship, whose verdict I simply accept. But in religion—in everything that concerns what has brought me here to-day, in reference to the questions as to whom and how I shall worship, as to who is to speak to me the final word on what I am to believe, as to what my outlooks will be when this life is over, and I am simply waiting for the door to open to usher me into the unseen, I have but one Master.

You may be my *helpers;* many of you who have never suspected it *have* been my helpers. I owe a debt to the writers of many books, who have set their mark upon me for ever. Men have touched my eyes and I have seen; have come to the cell where my own gloomy thoughts had imprisoned me, and unlocked the door, and I was free for ever. But I have never found those to be the men who are ambitious to be called masters; I have always found them willing to sit at the feet of any one who was fit to teach. Some there are, indeed, who intensely covet the name, who love to parade it, who never allow you to forget that they *are* masters; who covet to be called "Reverends" and "Right Reverends." No one calls me "Reverend" but he makes me wince. It is a poor, tinsel crown. But names do not crea'e facts; to be *called* master does not make you master. Helpers many there may be, but there is only one Master. "*One* is your Master, even the Christ." And I willingly acknowledge Him to be Master. He shall decide everything for me; He shall read life for me; I will accept His exposition of the riddle; He shall define duty for me, and I will cut life into the pattern which He has set before me, and line by line the future shall resolve itself into that which He has declared it is going to be.

The one Master—Christ; that is what I want to speak about—the one Master in religion.

I. AND FIRST: CHRIST IS MASTER ON THE GROUND OF HIS ABSOLUTE KNOWLEDGE OF EVERYTHING THAT LIES WITHIN THE DOMAIN OF RELIGION. The first thing that strikes you in Jesus is the absolute boldness with which He teaches—His daring, I might say. God cut the Ten Words which were to be the law for Israel upon the tables of stone without preface or apology. These were to be the lines by which every act of every man was henceforth to be measured. And Christ laid down *His* law with all the absoluteness and decisiveness of that; there is an audacity which is sublime in the tone in which He speaks. Moses declared this or that, but "*I* say unto you." "*I* am the Way, the Truth, and the Life." I am the Solution of life's mysteries; life is to be expounded in Me. "*I* am the Light of the world." The day breaks, the ghosts vanish, before Me.

Stay there for a moment.

1. His knowledge was absolute, complete, final. The knowledge of all others is only partial, hypothetical; beautiful as far as it goes, but never final. Real helpers; bits of the truth, sections of the truth, they know; the charm of their message is perfect as far as it goes; but they are only helpers, not masters.

The fact is, I do not expect any man to be more than a helper. I feel that a man has given me as much as I have the right to expect from him, if he cuts one idea into my mind, and makes it so clear and intelligible to me that I cannot forget it. Mr. Spurgeon was invaluable to me as far as he went. The perfect nineteenth-century Puritan, he dissolved seventeenth-century Puritanism in his blunt, rich, but utterly unromantic Anglo-Saxon brain, and you could never mistake as to his meaning. You had no liberty given you, so you felt as you listened to him, to re-analyze and re-read the Bible, and to ask curious questions about the construction of the Pentateuch, or the authorship of the various hymns in the grand Hebrew hymn-book which we call the Book of Psalms. To do so was an impertinence. What satisfied the Puritan fathers ought to satisfy you. You had no right to sigh for "fresh fields and pastures new." You had no business to be like Dr. Naanssen, the Norwegian explorer, who could not rest content, but must sail out, declaring that he meant to find the North Pole. Dr. Naanssen ought to have been satisfied with the Norwegian fiords; and English theologians ought to be satisfied with their fathers' theory of the atonement, and it is little short of irreverence for them to go peering into the future, and wondering whether the light of hope may not fall upon the destiny of the irredeemed, even beyond the bourn of death. But Mr. Spurgeon rang one clear message into the souls of thousands as no man in England for a hundred years had done—that man's only hope was Jesus Christ. For thirty years he rang the changes on this one theme, "Believe in the Lord Jesus Christ, and thou shalt be saved." He taught what he *saw*, but he never exhausted even that one rich verse.

Jonathan Edwards dissolved his soul into one doctrine, the sovereignty of God. To Jonathan Edwards man was the clay in the Potter's hand. The Potter moulded the clay into the form that pleased Him—to be a redeemed soul or a rejected soul as seemed good to Him; who was *he* to question the Potter's right? And he preached his awful doctrine, and terrified his hearers, and shook and shed tears whilst he preached it. The glorious, awful half-truth; but it was all he could see, and he preached what he saw.

Even the Apostles—Paul, Peter, John, James—and the author of the Epistle to the Hebrews, whoever he might have been—not one of these, taken by himself, delivered an absolutely complete and exhaustive gospel. Peter's gospel would often sound to men different from that of Paul. Peter frankly said that there were things in Paul "hard to be understood." I have no doubt that, if he ever tried to read the Epistle to the Colossians, he groaned over it as much as I have ever done. James, I should say, never could see the importance of Paul's constantly iterated doctrine of "justification by faith." What *he* was concerned about was that men should be rich in good works. The truth is, even the authors of these grand expositions of Jesus which we call the Epistles taught, each of them, just what he saw; but each was partial, incomplete, and, I have no doubt, would sometimes seem to the others to be deficient and one-sided. Each would shake his head at the others. Paul, a metaphysician, a romancist, a dreamer, an enthusiast, would often seem to every one of them, and especially to James, to exaggerate his favourite doctrine. "Justification by faith" might be even pernicious, might make people indifferent to morality—slow to work, to cleanse the sewers of life and to sweep the pestilence of sin out of the world. But Paul taught what he saw, and James taught what *he* saw; but both were incomplete. Scholars both, imperfect both.

"But one is your *Master*." The master carries the whole school, carries every teacher and every teacher's lesson in his own mind. The school includes the first Kindergarten lesson, and the highest problem in mathematics which the foremost scholar wrestles with; and the school is only the master's soul embodied. The infinitely varied glory of the mountain landscape—the hill, the valley, the rock, the meadow,—the solid granite foundation underlies them all. The rainbow flings its seven colours against the cloud as a background, but the seven colours are only the one ray of light resolved; remelt the colours, and they become one again—you have the simple ray of light. "I am *the Light* of the world," said our Lord. Every ray of light, every truth of every teacher, is in Christ. Paul is in Christ, and Peter also; James is in Christ, and also John. Teachers, rare, rich teachers, a radiant colour in the rainbow, every one of them; Christ is the *Light.* *Helpers,* all of them; Christ is the Master. "One is your Master, even the Christ."

2. Perhaps I ought to add one word to that—the *ease* with which He taught; the sense you always have, as you hear Him, that to deliver His message is a delight to Him. This is one proof that you can give that you are a master. The amateur-painter toils hard, corrects and recorrects his work, whilst he is trying to express the vision he has seen; the master-painter fixes his vision on the canvas with half a dozen strokes of his brush. Music is hard work to the beginner; he spells his way through his first lessons, picks them up note by note, catches momentary glimpses of the world in which the angels of harmony dwell, but it is weary climbing as yet. But music is a recreation to the trained musician; every key of his piano is alive, and to sit down to it is to relieve and refresh himself. So theology is a toilsome study to most of us; the ordinary theologian is a hard-worked man. Socrates—oh, Socrates was a theologian—worked hard at his argument, slowly wove his long line of syllogisms—none the less syllogisms because they were a series of questions and answers—until he had established his point, established it for himself as much as for his inquirer. Paul wrestled with his awful problems, "groaned, being burdened;" I should say grew lean and haggard over his great Epistles. Not so Jesus. There is no sign of toil or effort in Him as He unravels the abstrusest problems. He touched His subject, and it disclosed its secret; looked at the mystery, and it opened as a flower opens in the sunshine; struck it as the lapidary strikes the stone, and the stone divides, and its buried beauty flashes out. Teaching to Him was never a toil, never a weary inquiry, but

always a confident unveiling of the facts of His subject. This One was not an explorer, but Master.

3. To sit at the feet of such a One is a joy. At the feet of the Master who can unerringly tell us what we ought to do, who will unhesitatingly tell us what we must believe. The soul thirsts for such a One: the Master.

That explains a little the fascination which the Romish Church exercises over the minds of men. It is a perfect wonder to us, the men who find a home in that Church; men of brilliant intellects, keen thinkers; men who in science or literature form their own conclusions and acknowledge no one's authority as supreme; who would scorn the thought that because the Royal Society declared something to be a fact in science, they were therefore to accept it without any inquiry of their own. These men recognize the abuses of their great Church as much as anybody. They writhe against what often looks like senseless tyranny. I question whether Newman was ever perfectly happy in that Church. His soul must have abhorred many of its rules, and the Church never absolutely trusted him until very near the close of his life; but he submitted. There was nothing so terrible to him as uncertainty, and he finally accepted this Church, in which he imagined the concentrated wisdom of the ages spoke, as the supreme authority. Let the Church declare what he was to believe, and he would accept it, even when the doctrine looked half a lie and a libel upon God.

Protestants have very little room to boast over him. We are not very willing to acknowledge it, but we also like to have our creed determined for us. We like a denomination that speaks with authority. The majority in the Presbyterian Church of the United States at the present moment, have determined that they will not accept the responsibility of thinking for themselves. That is what the deposition of Dr. Briggs really means. Their fathers determined long ago in what sense the Bible was inspired, and they will abide by the decision of their fathers. It is an impertinence to doubt that Moses wrote the Book of Deuteronomy— the seventeenth century settled that once for all; and the nineteenth century is to sit like a child at the feet of the seventeenth. I would as soon sit at the feet of the pope as that. I would no more make any particular century or any particular assembly of divines my pope than the poor old Italian gentleman who shuts himself up as a prisoner in the Vatican. I would as soon have joined in that strange service last week, when Cardinal Vaughan and the grand dignitaries of his Church reinstalled Peter and Mary as the patron saints of England. Poor Mary! one of the most modest-minded women that ever lived—the *mother* of modesty—what must thou think of it, that millions in Christendom should make thee a mediator between them and the Saviour of the world! If anything can make thy heaven uneasy for thee, that does. Poor Peter! Story tells that thou wast crucified. Christendom might have refrained from crucifying thee afresh, by speaking as if it were well to have thee between it and the crucified Lord. Ye great thinkers of the earlier ages, men of the toughest, lithest intellects, who determined in drawing up your grand articles of faith that ye would go straight to Christ, that ye would acknowledge no authority but Him, who never allowed any one to be your Master but Him; we will prove that we are worthy of you by doing the same. We also will go to Christ. Here and there is a line in your creed that needs to be corrected—not many. I should not mind making the Assembly's Catechism my text-book in teaching my children, if you would only allow me to give my own exposition of it. We would not speak exactly as you did as to election and atonement, nor perhaps of the destiny of men in the hereafter; we would perhaps express it a little differently. But *your* Master is *our* Master; as you adored Him and swore fealty to Him, so will we. "*One* is your Master, even the Christ.*"*

II. AGAIN: CHRIST IS OUR MASTER ON THE GROUND OF THE ABSOLUTE PERFECTNESS OF HIS LIFE. What a man *is* lifts him higher than what he *knows*. We recognize the brilliant gifts of many who have never commanded our reverence.

1. Now, Jesus lived the noblest and most perfect life. That life has always fascinated men—fascinated even those to whom He has never been what He is to us, Master and Lord, "very God of very God." I have often thought of making a collection of the tributes that have been paid Him by those who have never acknowledged Him to be what we insist He is. John Stuart Mill paid Him the tribute of his unstinted admiration. Renan postponed every dream of his life to write the romance which he has called the "Life of Jesus." Strauss spent a long life in trying to prove that Jesus was a myth, but the myth became solider fact to him than his own existence; it exasperated and taunted him, and he could not let it be. The most brilliant English novelist of to-day has let us into his secret that his dream is to write a worthy Life of our Lord; everything he has done hitherto has been only a by-study and training of himself for that. Even Mr. Robert Buchanan— we all stand in awe of him—must make Jesus his subject, if it were only to prove how easily he can show that the

Galilæan has failed. Jesus has always been a study, the great subject that has fascinated the world. But to us He means much more than that. Not a mere intellectual or æsthetic study is He to us, but the incarnation of every virtue, the absolute expression of love and purity and every high grace—the divine law embodied, translated into plain human speech which we can understand. Purity, self-sacrifice, devotion to the weal of man,—we never think of these things in the abstract, *Jesus* is to us the absolute expression of what these things mean. I follow Him everywhere. I pray with Him on Olivet and in Gethsemane. I stand under His cross, and I say, "*This* is love." Christ did not merely teach; He *died*. His word may perplex me, but I understand that.

2. And now, the world will inevitably in the long run make the absolutely good one Master.

There is an old story which I love. It is the story of how the Welsh Church received Augustine—the Augustine who came to convert England in the days of the Saxons. I suppose you know that Wales was already Christian; that the Welsh driven into the hills—you have always been better fighters than we—had their Church whilst you were still heathen. But Augustine came, and the question arose in the Welsh Church as to how they should receive him. Was he sound in the faith? Should they make themselves one with him? He had sent them a message calling upon them to send some of their representative men to meet him; should they do so? In their perplexity they consulted one of the fathers of the Welsh Church, a venerable monk, and he said, "Determine whether you will identify yourselves with him not by what his *theological views* may be, but by what *he* is; is he a good man?" And the delegates went; and Augustine, with grand notions of his own dignity and position in the Church, received them sitting on a throne. And they said, "This man is swollen with pride; this man is not the Christian with whom we care to have any dealings;" and they withdrew. I wish Wales had remained true to that decision unto this day; that it had always said—I am sorry that it has not—" Let a man be a good man, and he shall be our brother, even though he may express his theological opinions in a different way from us." It is goodness alone, virtue, that it is fit to adore; in the long run it is the good man that becomes master.

Oh, you young fellows who have mothers whom you can revere, happy are you! The world sees nothing to startle it in her, but she embodies every grace for you. The proud entity which calls itself "society" never dreamt that it possessed anything to be proud of in her; but she is *your* Madonna, sweet and self-forgetful—God's proof set up in your home that the most perfect crown with which a woman can adorn herself is the crown of virtue and simple goodness. She is more to you than she would have been had she been a George Eliot and a Georges Sand rolled into one. Oh, you strong men who are beginning to count at fifty, how many you know whom you can believe in and reverence! You do no soul-homage to the merely clever man, who has long since proved that in the race for wealth and fame he can pass you and every competitor, and easily come in first; but to the man whose gifts, be they great or small, are being transmuted into the beauty of perfect goodness, whose face —oh, I know some such here, not the cleverest people by any means—whose face is becoming transparent, and God, like a light, shines behind it,—this is the man whom I revere.

I should like to have a grand picture-gallery placed absolutely under my control for once—to have it given me to decide as to what pictures should have a place in it. I would not forget John Ruskin and the ecstasy of his "Modern Painters;" I would remember Florence and Augustus Hare; but there is not one gallery arranged yet as it ought to be. I would have a few types of perfect physical beauty in it, of course; Raphael and Leonardo and Murillo should say, "This is what we mean by grace and loveliness." I would set the type of a perfectly drilled and developed human body there—physical strength and litheness; the Greek at his best. I would have him there. I would, if I could find it, have the face which should express the noblest type of intellect there. And then—for you have not set in every line yet—I would seek for the face which should express the most perfect *goodness*. There should be manliness in it, courage, pity, generosity, and the tenderest sympathy; ay, there should be healthy enjoyment of the sunshine and laughter and even humour of life in it. The face is not perfect without that; a monk's face is a poor face. And as I think of it, I find every one of them in one face and only one—the face of Christ. *That One* is the *Master*.

III. ONCE AGAIN: CHRIST IS MASTER ON THE GROUND OF WHAT HE HAS DONE FOR US. It is service more than all else that wins mastery; the world only worships those who have served it. And service touches its highest level in Christ. He has cleft the brain of evil, He has tapped the swamp of sin, and He will yet wipe the last ugly line out of the life of man.

1. What Christ did for us is nowhere fully expressed but in the Cross. I confess I always speak with bated breath

when I come to this. It means more to me than it ever did, but I am often half afraid to speak of it. I can look at it, I can worship nowhere as I can at the foot of the Cross. I can stand as Moses did under the brazen serpent and point to it; but I do not fancy that Moses' words were many then, and if we are wise we will not talk much here. I will only tell you this much now. Jesus had never told all that was in Him until He told it by the Cross; His work would have remained for ever unfinished had He shrunk from that.

How shall I put it? I have a delightful book, "Imago Christi." The author of the book tells us how he came to write it. He was engaged in writing another book on a subject that had fascinated him. He had been busy over it for years; but as he pursued his task, subsidiary thoughts came to him—thoughts that started off from the great subject that he had in hand; and this "Imago Christi" consisted of these side thoughts. So of this gospel. The Sermon on the Mount is in it; we shall never cut the last line into that. I look at it; it is a perfect jewel; I hold it up to the light, and some fresh hue for ever flashes out of it. The *miracles* are here. I understand many things through the miracles, and it is as revelations that I chiefly value them. They give hints to us as to what God's relations to the physical world are, as to how He works. But all these things are subsidiary matters, all these come by the way. The gospel, the divine message—that by which Christ told Himself—is the Cross. Nothing but the Cross has told us all that is in Him; the love, the pity, His pathetic yearning for us, His power to save.

2. And now, it is this that enthrones Christ in our hearts, that makes Him irresistible—the Master to whom we bind ourselves.

A famous Frenchman who had done much for his countrymen bethought himself once that he would invent a new religion for them—a religion which might replace the worn-out Christian faith, and satisfy every need of their nature. He began with a grand creed, consisting of what he imagined to be truths which could be verified. He composed a superb ritual which was to delight every æsthetic and emotional instinct in them. And then he set out through France on a preaching tour. Men came and listened, and went away laughing. He was painfully humiliated, for he was in dead earnest, and in any case not a conscious impostor; and in half despair he went to his friend Talleyrand, the subtle-minded, cynical old man. "Well, it is a pity," said Talleyrand; "it is wonderful, too; but I will tell you what you must do; you must go and get crucified, and rise again from the dead on the third day." Old Talleyrand was right. The world will never believe in one who cannot submit to be crucified, will never make him who cannot die for men absolute Master. Now, that is the One whom we preach; the Christ who died for you, who bore the burden of your sins, who so loved you that He could not lose you. Shall not *He* be your Master?

A GOOD REASON FOR NOT LEAVING CHRIST.

E—20

A GOOD REASON FOR NOT LEAVING CHRIST.

"To whom shall we go?"—JOHN v. 68.

Ay, to whom? For, to begin with—

I. TO SOME ONE WE MUST GO; SOME ONE WE MUST HAVE. Some one, I mean, who shall occupy for us a position analogous to that which Christ occupies—Master, Lord, the One whose word is final; some one who can solve for us life's riddle, expound its problems, put meaning into its disciplines; some one who can receive and shelter us when the storms of doubt and sorrow break upon us. No one tries to live without some one, or at least something—some "hiding-place from the wind, and covert from the tempest;" some "shadow of a great rock in a weary land;" some "rivers of water in a dry place." If you say to me, "Give up Christ," I ask, "Whom do you give me instead?" for some one I *must* have.

I begin there. Some one or something is absolutely necessary; you *must* have solid substance to build upon; you cannot build in space. The Romanes lecturer at Oxford the other day would say that the dearest articles of our belief are mere guesses, mere conjectures. We have created them; we believe in them because we like them.

But, conjectures or not, they are the very "bread of life" to us. Even he does not pretend that he can live without bread; there is an invincible spiritual hunger even in him, and he *must* have bread. To contribute something to the sum-total of human happiness, to make human life something richer, sweeter; to add one line to the beauty of the world—that pleasure he must have. Amidst the distractions and puzzles of this mysterious universe, he sets his foot down there; that at least is solid, and some solid foothold he must have. To serve the world is to him "the bread of life." It is not a very rich feast, but the man will not starve who sits down even to that table. The sermon is not a very cheerful one. If I were to offer it to you as my Sunday morning's message, you would imagine that I had got into a melancholy mood; there would not be much cheer in the message. But we *must* have something. To tell me to lift up my anchor and drive before the wind, to break up my moorings and simply drift "anywhere, anywhere, out of the world," is not enough;—*nay*, some anchoring ground I must have. Away from Christ? If you prove that I must, I *must;* but to whom shall I go? For *some one* you *must* give me.

Now wait for a moment there.

1. And first; religion is to me an absolute necessity; it is the one thing I *must* have. The measure of man's necessities depends upon the point from which you look at him. If he has no deeper necessities than those of his mere animal existence, then they are not very great; the earth can easily supply them. If life meant merely bread and—shall I say beer?—the problem the world presents would not be a very tragic one. We might easily solve that, and never have recourse even to a "strike."

A GOOD REASON FOR NOT LEAVING CHRIST. 53

God has made abundant provision for our physical necessities. Depend upon it, there is here "bread enough and to spare."

But let me speak of man's necessities for a moment. Physical necessities are a very small part of those necessities.

Intellectual necessities. The soul becomes hungrier than the body; ideas become more necessary than bread; to be intellectually starved becomes a greater privation than to be physically starved. I hunger for my book as I never hunger for my meals, and nothing but the sense that I have no right to worry the world keeps me from writing books as well as reading them. We grumble at the great cataract of books that is for ever thundering upon the world. My dear sirs, you might as well blame the chicken for pecking its way out of the shell, as blame the most commonplace book for being born. *You* are not bound to read it, but the poor author was bound to write it; that to him was an intellectual necessity.

Æsthetic necessities: the necessities that express themselves in art and music. I once saw a collection of the most primitive musical instruments in the world—harps of only two or three strings, primitive organs and pianos, guitars and lutes; the countless contrivances which man has devised to translate his deepest joys and brightest visions. There was something pathetically touching in them to me. Better proofs that music is a necessity to man—that the hunger for melody is in his heart—than this noble instrument behind me. I spent some hours last week in our Royal Academy. To paint those pictures was a *necessity* to the hundreds whose work you had there before you. No *great* picture there, no picture to make the year memorable in the story of art; but scores of pictures to prove that the instinct of beauty is strong in this generation—that Englishmen have discovered the divinity in Nature's face, and the pathos that lies in common scenes and common life. To lose its art would be a real deprivation to England.

More than that. Things that our fathers never dreamt of as necessities have become necessities to us. Every village in the kingdom is getting to demand its public library; the public park and public baths are getting to be counted as our common rights. The community which does not possess them will soon begin to count itself as wronged. As man rises his necessities rise.

But there is one thing that has clung to him more tenaciously than anything else—nay, that is not the way to put it—that has been more persistently a part of him than anything else; it is his passion for religion. Art is born late; the passion for knowledge only gradually grew in him; *religion* has always lain at the roots of his heart, and he never outgrows it. The gross ideas that are inevitably part and parcel of it at the outset, the ignoble or childish notions, the superstitions that cling to it,—he disentangles himself from these; the grave-clothes of an ugly theology he lays aside, but the necessity for religion grows upon him. More necessary than the bread he eats, than the air he breathes; the life of his life. You may dismiss him out of the Christian temple if you like; you may prove to him that its foundations are undermined, that it is collapsing and coming down about his head; he will look back to it with pathetic wistfulness and ask, "To whom shall we go?" *Religion* he must have.

2. Then, this religion must be incarnated in a person.

A GOOD REASON FOR NOT LEAVING CHRIST. 55

"To *whom* shall we go?" Not "*what*," but "*whom*." The object of our trust—our refuge—must be one to whom we can tell our tale, at whose feet we can sob out our sorrows; in the words of the apostle, "who can be touched with the feeling of our infirmities." No mere text-book in which you have classified my duties, and told me what I must be and do under every conceivable circumstance, is enough. Mr. Herbert Spencer has just published the last volume of his "System of Ethics;" his exposition of "duty," of the laws upon which duty rests, the principles upon which you are always to determine what you ought to do. There is no man in Europe but himself who could have written the book. But it has a most pathetic preface—the saddest bit of writing that has been penned by a great man for many days. He questions very much whether he has been of any great help to the world—whether you have done much for a man simply because you have shown him what he ought to do; and he is right. Let Mr. Herbert Spencer say what he likes, man wants some one upon whose bosom he can sob, to whom he can tell the sorrow that is choking his heart, upon whom he can lean when the world is reeling under his feet.

You remember the old Greek story of the sculptor working at his marble, engrossed with the figure which he was with every stroke of his hammer lifting out of the block; fascinated by it, having forgotten everything in the beauty which grew upon him as he worked. Gradually the figure stirred, breathed; the eyes opened, and it looked back into the face of the sculptor. His soul's passion and hunger for the beautiful thing, his desire and homage to it, lifted it into life. That is a very old story; it is the story of religion. To Gautama, the father of Buddhism, God was only a beautiful idea, a passionless, emotionless Being, who felt nothing, knew nothing, whose consciousness in any case was only a dream. But to the Buddhist of to-day God is the God of pity, the God who sympathizes with the sorrows and distresses of men, the God who gives His hand to help us. The Buddhist has looked so wistfully into the face of his idea that it has become alive. The Positivist insists that there is no personal God. Categorically examine him, drive him into a corner, insist that he shall define the words which he has borrowed from the Christian vocabulary, and you will find that all he means by God is a number of noble ideas, a sublime galaxy of virtues—self-denial, purity, courage, the aggregate of service rendered by the noblest souls; a grand name for goodness—nothing more. But when Mr. Frederic Harrison begins to talk, his dead God becomes alive under his hand, and you half wonder whether he is not a Primitive Methodist or a Salvation Army evangelist.

I will tell you what it is. I saw a picture the other morning—a picture of the Foolish Virgins at the Bridegroom's door, craving to be admitted. You do not see the Bridegroom, you only see a hand; but there is a crowded story in that hand. That hand positively speaks. There is reproach in it; it says, "Why did you neglect your opportunity?" There is the stern rejection of them in it; there is the strong determination of one who can do terrible things and punish in it. It is all in that hand. It is not a law of nature that punishes; it is one who thinks, feels; one who has been wounded, grieved, hurt; it is a Personality. And so I say of the religion that cheers you. It is not merely a code of ethics, a perfect exposition of the laws of morality; it is not a mere galaxy of beautiful ideas and of

A GOOD REASON FOR NOT LEAVING CHRIST. 57

sublime ideals. There is a *hand* in it; there is help in it. You *grasp* the hand, and the hand grasps *you*. The pity of a Father's heart is in the hand, the quiver of sympathy—love, pardon, help; there is everything in the *hand*. Ay, in the religion that can cheer, there must be a *hand*; the Saviour must be a *Person*.

That first; and now, secondly—

II. WE HAVE ALL THAT, FOR WE HAVE CHRIST. Our Saviour is not an abstract idea, not a system of ethics, not a sublime scheme of morality, but a "THOU." We have learnt to love Him, we have absolute faith in Him. Christendom is built upon Him; with all the passion of love we adore and delight in Him.

Now, will you think of Him? I know you are always willing when I say "we will consider *Him*." Not that we can exhaust Him, and say everything there is in Him. Dr. Fairbairn's lately published book, "Christ in Modern Theology," is a brave attempt to expound Him; but Dr. Fairbairn candidly confesses that it is only an attempt. But we have some certainties; there are some things in Him that are absolutely clear to us, and about which we are absolutely sure.

1. First: He has "the words of eternal life." That is, the true life, the divine life, the life of God; for that is always the meaning of the word "eternal" when John uses it. But "eternal" means "immortal," you say? To be sure it does. Everything "eternal" *is* "immortal;" that is, everything that is true, everything that shares in the life of God, is immortal. If you are true as God is true, if you have the life of God in you, you are immortal as God is immortal. Our Lord never set about *proving* that the good man was immortal; His words always implied that he was *necessarily*

immortal *because* he was good; you can no more conceive of his ceasing to be than you can conceive of God ceasing to be.

Now, "*Thou* hast the words of eternal life." And oh, what a life we see it to be, when Christ descants upon it! What a bewitching thing science is when you get a genuine scientist to expound it! The man who cannot interest you with his science—depend upon it, he does not know it. The botanist or the geologist has no right to be dull. Professor Dewar at the Royal Institution the other day talked like a troubadour. His lecture or exposition—you may call it what you like—was the severest science, but it was a perfect romance. You felt that the only man who had made a right use of his life was the man who had been working at the chemist's or the physicist's crucible. It was poetry, it was music.

I once heard John Ruskin. I never could draw. I remember the drawing-master's scorn of a famous attempt at a picture I once made, though that was nearly forty years ago now. But I half felt, when I heard John Ruskin, that the one mistake of my life had been that I had not made painting the work of my life. I *knew* I could paint as I listened to him. In any case, I understood for the first time how prodigally beautiful the world was in which God had placed me to live. I got to understand that the New Jerusalem which John saw in the Revelation might be realized anywhere, might be realized even in London, might be set up in St. Giles or Whitechapel. I saw that the "tree of life" grew everywhere; that "the river of the water of life" might flow through every city slum, might go singing before every door. What a revelation it was! It was the born artist talking about art.

And " eternal life "—the true life, the brave life, God's

life; the life of love and purity, the life of self-denial and noble patience, the life that gives itself, and finds its highest joy—nay, finds *itself* in giving itself; the life that bears the burdens of others, that soothes the sorrows, mitigates the woes, lightens the cares of others—what am I talking about? —the Cross, the life that spoke in the Cross, told itself in the blood that was shed upon the accursed tree—*that* is the "eternal life." And when Christ expounds it, it is an enchantment, it is perfect music, it is the song of the divine heart; it fascinates one. I also can bear the Cross, can die. Fill us, O God, fill us with the life that is in Thee! *That* is the only life, the "eternal life."

2. Again: there is a personal and indelible relationship between our Lord and us. "Go away!" said Peter. "Leave Thee!" We have tasted of the life that Thou givest, the life that is to be found only in Thee. Go? Break the ties that bind us to Thee? Never.

Experiences shared together deepen friendship, strengthen its ties. You have known each other, helped each other, stood by each other in trouble, and every test to which you have been put has bound you closer together. Knowledge of each other even deepens *love*. You loved each other five and twenty years ago; you have blessed God every day of the five and twenty years that you ever met; you have no doubt that it was God brought you together. The sweet light dwells upon those divine days—*your* Paradise. *You* were a poet then; there was not a colour in the sky bright enough, not a song in the woodland that could tell the rapture that was in you. Excuse another picture illustration—dear me, it is beginning to dawn upon me that the Exhibition was, after all, richer than I knew; it was the picture of a dignified old couple—a noble old man, a veritable patriarch, and his charming sunny-souled wife who had been his companion for so many years, who had "clomb the hill" with him and shared "monie a canty day" with him—celebrating their golden wedding. Their sons and daughters are there with them, and the grandchildren are taking happy part in the celebration. The brave pair loved one another fifty years ago, but—and you can see it in the face of each—not so deeply or fervently as they did that morning. And listen: I loved Christ almost as far back as I can remember. He was with me when I was a boy; with me in the hour of temptation and in the agony of sin; and with me in the crucial, terrible, but blessed hour of repentance. He has been with me in trouble; I have sobbed on His bosom; He has cheered me when my heart was breaking. Right back to the days of my boyhood, at every turn of the road, I see *Him*, and every hour has made Him dearer. "Go away" from Him? Nay. You must show me some one who can do infinitely more for me than He can before I will ever go away.

And now, lastly—

III. IF WE LEAVE HIM—THAT IS, MUST LEAVE HIM—for we will not leave Him until we *must*—TO WHOM SHALL WE GO? Two things I have fully determined.

1. First: that to whomsoever I go, he must be a genuine *Saviour*. It is of no use your insisting that I do not *need* a Saviour. It is of no use your trying to persuade the hungry man that he is not hungry, that he only imagines himself to be hungry. It is of no use your telling me to respect and honour myself, and work out my own salvation. I have painfully tried, and the story of my attempts is a story of dreary failure, and despair fills my heart as I think of it. A Saviour I *must* have; a better Saviour even than

Jesus, before I leave Him; a Saviour who will meet my necessities better, who can feed me with healthier bread, who is a more genuine physician than He. Others may say that they need no Saviour—at least, not the Saviour that I need. I refuse to judge any man; "let every man be persuaded in his own mind." I will even acknowledge that the lives of men who reject the truths that are my inspiration, which gird me with strength, are often pure and lovely and of good report. It is not for me to say that they are racked with hunger, wounded with sorrows, haunted with a sense of loneliness to which they will not confess. What right have I to say, that because I need a plain road and many helps by the way, that they do? I have seen a man walk before now on a rope stretched a hundred feet above the ground—indeed, we have all read of the man who ventured on a rope stretched across the Falls of Niagara, and whose nerve never failed him, though hungry death lay in the deeps below; but the majority of us will choose to have the solid earth under our feet, nevertheless. So there are men who walk the slender rope of the many substitutes for Jesus which are offered to-day; but as for me, I will remain on the solid road which He has provided for me. I will make no experiments. This is a plain path; no one has ever walked thereon and perished. That is enough for me.

2. Put to the test, every other Saviour than Jesus fails. We have all of us made experiments. The story of the Prodigal Son repeats itself in many forms. Many leave the father's house, not to plunge themselves into sin, but from sheer love of intellectual excitement. Just as the lad leaves the home where he has been so tenderly nurtured, where love has lavished its richest devices upon him, to try the adventures and excitements of sea-life. He has read so

much about them that they have become a fever of longing in him, and he must try them for himself. Life at home is tame and uninteresting, and he will at least taste these. So many leave their fathers' faith, not because they have been disappointed in Jesus, because they have tried Him and found Him wanting, but simply tempted by the roving spirit in them, and they have gone out to see what other faiths had to offer, what other Saviours professed to be able to do for man. Some of us have sat for a while at the feet of every modern prophet in turn. We know what Positivism has to give; we have tried to make a feast of the crumbs that fell from its table. We have listened and have been half fascinated by the materialist, who declares that his *work* is food enough for him, and that he can satisfy every hunger upon that. The story of Laurence Oliphant has been our own, some of us. Our first wanderings were mere experiments, an exciting bit of romance. But real hunger came some day, and when it came we found these fashionable substitutes for the gospel to be poor "apples of Sodom," which filled our mouth with ashes.

I can imagine fire to be so well painted as to deceive the eye for a moment, and I can imagine myself drawing near it to warm myself thereby. I have even read of the evolutionists' pet—the ape—sitting shivering before the painted fire, and wondering at the mystery of a fire that gave no heat. We have risen a little above that, at any rate; painted fire cannot deceive us for more than a moment. And so we may have been deceived by the many substitutes for Jesus offered us, but it was only for a moment. Positivism is a painted fire; materialism is a heap of cold, grey ashes. Neither of them can deceive us long; we shall not attempt o warm our shivering spirits over them.

THE BUILDING UP OF CHRISTIAN MANHOOD.

THE BUILDING UP OF CHRISTIAN MANHOOD.

> "But ye, beloved, building up yourselves on your most holy faith, praying in the Holy Ghost, keep yourselves in the love of God, looking for the mercy of our Lord Jesus Christ unto eternal life."—JUDE 20, 21.

THE older we get—at least, after we have passed out of the regions of youth—the more we wish to reduce life, its laws, its rules, its aims, to simplicity. We like the *author* who can sum up his argument in his last chapter, who can gather up the threads, and in a few strong, well-defined sentences tell us what all that has gone before means. We admire the *man* who, as the last chapter opens, gathers the argument of his life within conciser and conciser limits, and who does it—and that is the admirable thing—without becoming sour or cynical. There is a time to dream, a time to make experiments, a time for holiday-making. But a man comes to put his dreams from him—they are not feasible; he returns from his many excursions—there is no knowledge, nor happiness, nor anything that can beautify or bless life to be found in that direction. And this is the fine man—the man who can put away his dreams, cease from experiments, without one unkind thought of that through which he has passed, or a sneer for those who are repeating the process. He simply gathers up the threads of life, keeps close to its main issues; gathers *himself* together too, that he may carry life up to its highest possibilities.

So also of the gospel. The longing for the *simple* gospel comes as life moves on. Do not mistake me. I am not referring to the indolence which wants to make salvation easy, not to the platitudes of theology which to so many are merely convenient excuses for not thinking: but to the desire to meditate upon its main truths, to get hold of its essence, to bring life into harmony with its chief aims; to give our strength—strength of thought, strength of inquiry, strength of striving—to the one idea in it towards which everything tends.

Now, the Bible is a great book. It would be difficult to say what the subject is which the Bible does not touch. To make a small selection of subjects is simply to be untrue to the Bible. And people who expect to have some one or two pet ideas—which are to be found in the Bible, to be sure—always in every sermon, who pride themselves that they believe as others do not believe in the inspiration of the Bible, who always insist upon having these few ideas in the front, logically or illogically, reasonably or unreasonably; there if they happen to be there, or dragged there if they are not there;—they simply prove that they do *not* believe in the inspiration of the Bible—the inspiration of the whole of it. The book is a great world, and he who preaches the whole Bible will preach a great many subjects, and somebody must be always content to have his pet idea left out. But sometimes—to-day, shall I say? This is a gathering of the Churches; many opinions meet here to-day. It would be a wonderful meeting, if we could get every sermon preached

THE BUILDING UP OF CHRISTIAN MANHOOD. 67

by every one here during the last twelve months to come up and be analyzed—our poor weary and burdensome sermons as well as the strong and brilliant ones which made everybody marvel! "Many thoughts of many minds." We should see, perhaps, that the most hopeless idea would be the idea that the ministers of England might be all beaten into one pattern. But we may ask, What has been the essence of it all, the sum of all the preaching? Suppose we gather up the threads; what has it all meant? what is the underlying idea? upon what should we concentrate our thinking and striving? Listen: "Building up yourselves on your most holy faith, praying in the Holy Ghost, keep yourselves in the love of God, looking for the mercy of our Lord Jesus Christ unto eternal life." *That is it.* And let that be our subject—the building up of Christian manhood, and the conditions under which it is built up.

As stated here the subject includes three things.

I. FIRST OF ALL, THE FAITH. "Building up yourselves on your most holy faith." I might say broadly, no splendid man was ever built up, no fine character was ever formed, no grand enterprise was ever created, but by a positive belief—a FAITH. And definite belief is the thing from which Christian manhood starts.

Now, to build upon the "faith"—

1. We must first have a clear notion of what the "faith" is. (1) That is, to begin with, we must distinguish between the faith and accretions to the faith; between the tree and the parasites that have entwined themselves about the tree; between the rock and the sand which has accumulated upon the rock. It is not too much to say, at least, that the accretions have been considerable, and one of the most serious parts of one's business is to remove

accretions and to get back to the original. I find it one of the most difficult things to keep myself wide-awake, always vigilant, never to allow myself to be deluded to confound the faith with *accretions to* the faith. We may persuade ourselves that we are jealous of the honour of the faith, that we are its champions, whilst we are the champions of the very things that obscure, mar, distort, maim, limit, cripple it.

We are sadly afraid of some of the intellectual movements of the day—intellectual movements that are felt in the Church as well as out of it. We are for ever talking of "negative theology," of destructive criticism. These are demolishing the old gospel. Do not let us give way to wild talk. I will tell you what it is. A very few years ago one of the noblest cathedrals in England—the one most familiar to me—used to be habitually spoken of with contempt. Its nave columns were huge masses of commonplace material overlaid with plaster. But some one, one day, had the wisdom to dig into this plaster, and lo! beneath were noble columns of exquisite marble. Nobody said, that I know of, that it would be desecration to destroy this venerable plaster, and soon, *very* soon, it had vanished; and now you have the original columns, an honour to the genius that designed them and the generosity of the past generation that built them. That is all that is going on in these days. Destruction, do you say? Nay, it is restoration, not destruction; it is the bringing back of the temple of divine truth to its original design and proportions, the bringing out again of the lines of its pristine beauty. That is all. There is much noise and dust, but we will not be foolish; there is nothing going but plaster. Let it go. "*Contend* for the faith once delivered unto the saints;"

THE BUILDING UP OF CHRISTIAN MANHOOD. 69

but zeal, passion, enthusiasm, is wasted in fighting for additions to the faith; in proving the divinity of plaster, and contending for the sacredness of human obscurations of the ineffable glory.

(2) Then, secondly, we must grip the Faith, understand the Faith, present it clearly and vividly to ourselves. Now, do not make a mistake. To understand a thing does not necessarily mean to remove all mystery from it. The most accomplished scientist in the world does not profess to understand nature in the sense that he has absolutely expounded nature. To understand the gospel does not mean to eliminate mystery from it, but it does mean to state it clearly to yourself. You cannot build upon mist, you cannot grow strong on mere sentiment, you cannot foster Christian manhood upon vague emotionalism. If your faith is to have anything to do with the making of you, the first thing is to *state* it clearly and distinctly to yourself.

There are two radically different conceptions of religion. Speaking broadly, the word "Protestantism" covers the one, and "Romanism" covers the other. Protestantism has its weaknesses, its limitations; it often requires to be supplemented by something else. But Protestantism is strong in this—it believes in stating its faith clearly to itself; it distrusts what it cannot thus state to itself. Protestantism is the religion of the soul when it is wide-awake and determined to play no tricks upon itself. The other is the religion of sentiment; the religion that expresses itself in masses, and oratorios, and the vague aspirations of architecture; the religion of a soul which is only half-awake; the religion of twilight. You muse, you dream, "whether in the body or out of the body" you cannot tell; and sweet music plays upon a soul in which the intellect has been sent to sleep and only the emotions listen. That is Romanism. To be sure, it *has* a theology—there is a side of it that speaks to the intellect; but the people, the many, have nothing to do with that. The grand church, the imposing mass, the noble music,—*that* is what the many have to do with.

Now, there are signs, many signs—I am not a panic-monger, but you cannot be blind—that the tendency of much in the religious life of England just now, and that in more Churches than one, is towards this religion of vague emotion, and away from the religion of clear statement. There is a sense in which England can never go over to Rome; the pope—and we may say, "God bless the old man!" in passing—can never again be recognized as pontiff or sovereign spiritual authority; but we can go over to Rome whilst we never acknowledge the authority of Rome. And the whole set of the tide seems sometimes to be in that direction. You hear everywhere, "Oh, religion is not a matter of clear and positive belief; it does not matter much what you *think*, it is what you *feel*. Oh, I do not care for the sermon, I do not go to hear that; I like the music, I like the soothing effect, the mesmeric touch of the service. I do not care what the man preaches. It is not good behaviour to go out when the sermon begins, or I would go out; as it is, I do not listen." It is in this sense that England is going over to Rome, in the sense that the Romish conception of religion is getting hold of it. Now, come back. To *build* upon your most holy faith you must know it, state it to yourself, clearly understand it, grip it.

2. Again: To build upon the faith, we must be continually carrying it further. The circle of Christian truth

is a wide one; the applications of every Christian fact are endless, the sweep of every Christian doctrine is infinite. And we must be carrying every Christian truth continually further; we must search out all the ramifications of it, know every bypath, roam through every field. This implies, first, that we must never cease from fresh, ever-renewed, and expectant study of it. We must be always ready for surprises, and never dream that we have come to the end of it. It is very difficult to behave yourself in the presence of people who will at any time glibly retail the great facts of the gospel, and say, "I have no need to reconsider those; I settled them long ago. I ask no curious question." I have heard people speak of mountain scenery. I have asked them, "Do you know Snowdon?" "Oh yes!" "And, pray, how often have you ascended Snowdon? Or"—for there is something more important than merely to ascend to the summit; it is quite as necessary to live at the foot—"how long have you lived within sight of it?" "Oh, I saw the mountain once; spent a day in the neighbourhood once. I ascended it, too. Oh yes, I know Snowdon!" "Ascended it once, saw one aspect of it, and you know it! Why, you must live there to know it. You must watch the mountain in a hundred moods. You must see it trace its outline against a cloudless sky; see it wrapped in mist, and clothing itself in infinite suggestions of mystery. You must see it when spring creeps up its sides, and when winter has set its throne of snow upon its summit; you must see it sleeping in a trance of summer heat, and hear the shout of its children when the floods are out. *Then* you may say that you know it." So of the faith. We cannot master this once for all. We cannot sum up its doctrines, settle them, and have done with them. We must pitch our life before them. We must live out every experience in their presence, and see how they look, when the servants of good fortune stand every morning at your door, asking, "What shall we do for thee to-day?" when storms hustle one another through your lot, and the hurricane seems to be sweeping every comfort beyond recall; when health is abundant and the work is easy, and everything prospers which you touch; when the strain is killing you, and your mind has lost its nerve and elasticity, and you dread what may happen. We must know the gospel under every light and every aspect; know the fruit the tree of life bears every month of the year; know the angle at which the light catches it every hour of the day, from the rising to the setting of the sun.

Once again; and I say it lest I should be misunderstood. I have spoken of active study; let me add—

3. The power to be passive is as requisite as the power to be active. We must be able not only to be busy, but to wait; to give ourselves up to the gospel as well as wrestle with it for the possession of its great secret. Aggressiveness is as often defeated as not. The gospel must *give* its secret; it cannot be wrested from it. It must disclose itself; you cannot compel it or take it by a rush. It is of no use to make an intellectual assault upon it. There are subtle beauties, finer shades of meaning, in every gospel truth; you cannot force these, but they will disclose themselves, if you can wait and give them time.

My brother-ministers, I hesitate very much to address myself directly to you; but you understand what I mean. How often do we go to the study; we make a direct attack upon some great truth which has haunted us, and which we have told ourselves we *must* understand! But attack is

THE BUILDING UP OF CHRISTIAN MANHOOD. 73

of no use; it refuses to give itself, and we fling it down, and rush away from it, and in sadness which is half resentment say, "I can make nothing of it." Stay there; whatever you do, you must not go. It is not the time *to do;* it is the time to be quiet. Just listen. There is a story in every great picture which you cannot master in a hurry; you must lend yourself to it, give yourself up to it in active passiveness. There are subtle voices in the air which the human ear has not yet been trained to catch. Science is getting to be the handmaid of poetry. The atmosphere *is* full of fairies, and the legend of voices heard upon the midnight air will be yet translated into the text-books of the dogmatic young prophetess which has laughed so mercilessly at visions and dreams. And so there are glories here which you must sit down to see; quieter tones in the voice of Jesus which you will never hear until you cease from your hurry and distraction, until sometimes you give up even your work, your most Christian work. There are spiritual processions in the Bible, but you must cultivate the quickest spiritual perception, or you fail to see them; the air throbs with angelic voices, but you must *hush* your soul and be quiet even from work and service, or you never catch them. That much for the "Faith." And now, secondly—

II. THE SPIRITUAL ATMOSPHERE IN WHICH YOU LIVE. That, in the next place, determines your progress in Christian manhood. "Praying in the Holy Ghost, keep yourselves in the love of God."

1. "Keep yourselves in the love of God." There are many aspects in which the love of God is looked at in these Scriptures; and I think this is as remarkable as one of them—that to be "*in* the love of God," to live in the constant sense of it, is one of the indispensable conditions

of spiritual growth, that Christian manhood is impossible without. I could make nothing of that at first; but I very soon saw that it was so, and that the world is full of analogies of it.

To begin with, we make nothing of the truths of the gospel; they never become more than opinions, never become spiritual strength, are never transmuted into food, health, spiritual robustness, joy; they are never vitalized, unless you live in the love of God, and breathe it as the atmosphere of your life. You delight in your garden. Cultivate the taste. A garden is a means of grace; the company of growing things is as humanizing as the study of literature. You go and look at your plants. You see that they have everything they need. They are set in the right soil, they have the due amount of moisture, they have sufficient heat. But you forget them; you let the fire go out, and you go in a week and find your favourites—full of life to-day, every one of them having stolen its special secret from the sun—find them all dead. Or you remove them into a cellar. You give them everything, even heat, but you shut out the light from them, and you go and visit them by-and-by, and find that you have a collection of ghosts—pale, colourless caricatures of plants. Nay, if you want them to grow, and you would delight in their beauty, you must give them warmth and sunlight. And so of this. You can make very little of the Bible—the majority of men will make nothing of it—unless you keep yourselves in the warmth and light of God's love. You take every rule of conduct in the Book, and you try to live them out one by one; you shut your lips and determine, exert all your force of will, keep yourself tied to the grim angel of duty like a prisoner tied to his guardian policeman; but you can make nothing of them. They simply stupefy you, and, dull and discouraged, you shrink into yourself.

I will make a confession. Love is a necessity to me. I have no courage to try to live without it. To preach law, to set clearly before myself the lines of duty, is not enough for me. I pine for love, and I am weary of the constant reiterating of the sacredness of law, the majesty and dignity of law, and the obedience which I must render it. I am ready to protest sometimes; everybody insists upon preaching law to you. I become a guest at a house, and there is a card hung up on your bedroom wall which practically says, "Life is ticketed off into a distinct number of rules in this house; we live by the clock here; meals are served with the regularity of the tides; the sun rises according to signals which it receives from this house;" and from that moment I am miserable. I begin to read, and the moralist gives me his code of ethics, his inexorable ten commandments, his two tables of stone—ay, stone, rigid, unbending—and says, "There, my dear sir, you are equipped for life now; keep these, and you can defy the universe." The political economist comes and quotes his infallible axioms, and says, "These are the conditions upon which the well-being of the world is to be realized; give strict heed to these, and you will be an heroic man and benefactor of your race." The scientist puts on an air of severe wisdom, and says, "My dear friend, life is easy; obey every law of your being, and it shall be well with you—*law* is the one thing to be heeded." Quite so, gentlemen. Preach on; I will try to remember. Great law, sublime law! Thou art deified! Omnipotent law, stern law, grim-faced, sublime law! But I am sick and tired of hearing of thee; if I dared, I would almost say I hated thee. Majestic, beautiful, *terrible;* if I were strong and heroic, and never made a mistake, the gospel concerning thee might be very pleasant to hear. But I want something more to be preached to me to live, to be strong and courageous thereby; I want warmth; I want sunshine; I want the sense that God's benediction is upon me; I want *love*. Everything then, the sternest command, the hardest duty—becomes food to your soul, and you grow and become robust thereby. The health of God, the deep peace of God, sinks into your soul, and there is nothing in life that can beat you.

And now grant me a moment's digression. I want to have a word with you, my brother-ministers. For the moment I see no one but you.

Brethren, none need so much to live and move and have their being in this love as we. We brood over mysteries—I suppose this is natural—we simmer in our own thoughts the whole week long. The temperament which has led us to preach, makes us liable to depression and melancholy. Mephistopheles pursues no one so relentlessly as he pursues us. No one has so many spectral thoughts; life hurts no one at so many points. The ideas that are supposed to be the special discovery, the special contribution of this generation to the mental wealth of the world, the ideal substitutes for the God and Father of our Lord Jesus Christ, comfort no one so little as they comfort us. I could blacken the blackest words that were ever spoken, I could outsneer the most melancholy pessimist that ever lived, when I have lost the warmth of the divine love. No pessimist is so pessimistic as the preacher who is a pessimist; and we bring all our pessimism out on a Sunday morning. We search out all melancholy texts; we describe a circle around " Man is born to trouble, as the sparks fly upward." Life to our people has been hard all the week, and we drag them over harder and stonier roads on the Sunday. Don't! For God's sake, don't! It is a crime, it is a sin. Our thoughts should be visions; there should be a breeze in our words, a sheen upon our raiment; men should feel the fresh air of the Delectable Mountains lift their hair.

I remember spending a day in one of the loveliest spots in Europe. Nature dipped her hand deep into her treasury of resources, used her most exquisite materials that day. A range of noble mountains covered with eternal snow pierced the sky. Law was there; force in its most tremendous personifications was there. There were scars upon the mountain's brow that had taken ten thousand years to write, great trees upon the mountain-side which the avalanches of last winter had snapped like matchwood. But the sun caught the whole scene before disappearing. The black precipices relaxed into a tremor of purple. The snow caught fire and glowed as if preparing to vanish. But the sun went, and the mountains set their awful countenances hard again. The snow was cold, and a chill breath blew across the valley. The scene was awful, terrible, grim, and it was pleasant to go in and shut it all out. So, men talk of the majesty and grandeur of God's law, expatiate upon the divine order. Oh yes! divine order; but it is too awful, too overpowering for me. I shrink into myself and cannot stand up before it. When the light of love is away, it is a cold, terrible, disheartening world. Oh, men and women, life takes the courage out of the bravest of us sometimes! Throngs of difficulties confront us, and refuse to stir out of our path. Life looks like a combination of adamantine laws not one of which will *give* to make our work an iota the easier. And then the many who depend upon us come. Expositions of Providence are demanded of us, as if *we* knew everything. It was only as if it were yesterday that I was called upon to comfort a circle of breaking hearts. I had to bury a charming girl of twenty, who had been an angel in her home—the third of that very age whom I had had to bury from that family in five short years. Comfort! *I* needed comfort. A word could have made an infidel of me. But we pass up into the mountain. The love, the tenderness, the compassion, the grace, the mercy, catch our faces. Life shines, work shines; the dingiest work becomes radiant; hope, like a rainbow, spans the blackest sorrow. The hardest word in this Book blossoms; it steals into your soul like a strain of music that has wandered from Paradise; you forget that it is a command, and your soul bursts into rapture. You rest in God, and your joy is absolute, complete, perfect.

2. "Praying in the Holy Ghost." Praying. A thorny question, you say. Not at all. In the connection in which I am speaking of it now, no argument is needed. I am talking of spiritual growth, and no one believes, whatever else he believes, that there can be spiritual growth without it. There have been plenty of controversies about prayer, but there never has been any controversy about this, that to grow and to pray must always go together.

For just think. Prayer keeps the sense of God and heaven alive in the soul; it keeps up the bond of connection between earth and heaven. I pray, and heaven and all the help of heaven keep near me; I cease to pray, and heaven removes itself, becomes dim and unreal; and when I read a sceptical book, or a sceptical companion insinuates a doubt, or some wild half-delirious soul bitterly flings itself against the truths which I profess to believe—if he only knew it, his rage being only a cry for help—I am ready to be the chief disbeliever of all. Heaven has vanished, God is dead, there is no hereafter.

I go into a man's house—this is not altogether fiction—and he begins to moan over the wretched climate of this land. The sun never appears. Dark and dull and depressing; there is no light by which a man may do his work. I look around me, and lo, every window is dust-covered, no sunlight can pierce it, and I say, "My dear sir, excuse me, but suppose you begin there; clean these windows to start with. The sun does shine sometimes, even in England; be ready when it shines to receive its glorious wealth of light."

And so here. I am ready to contend a great deal for prayer; I am ready to contend for some things which prayer effects that once I was not very sure about. But in any case, this I am sure of—it keeps the windows of the soul clean, it facilitates the entrance of God into the soul, it puts the soul in touch with all spiritual realities. If there *be* a God, He *must* reveal Himself to the soul that prays; if there be an eternal world, pray, and you must pray yourself into the midst of it. Come here. Stand amid the wealth of this glorious revelation. Would you understand it? Would you have the light of it fill your soul? Would you miss nothing of it? Would you be inspired by it, have it shine through you and through everything that pertains to you, and transfigure all? Would you have it irradiate your work and change the fashion of your countenance? Then *pray*, PRAY; "PRAY WITHOUT CEASING." "BE INSTANT in prayer."

III. OUR GROWTH DEPENDS UPON THE SOUL'S OUTLOOKS,

THE INSPIRATIONS THAT LIE FOR US IN THE FUTURE.
"Looking for the mercy of our Lord Jesus Christ unto eternal life."

There is a famous essay which I am never tired of reading—Emerson's "Prospects"—the outlooks of life. I went the other day to see a member of my congregation who is a great sufferer—a woman who is half her life, three-fourths of her life, a prisoner. I condoled with her, sympathized with her. "Come up into my little room," she said. "There, sit in that window. When the torture begins, when I am worried and weary, when the fog gets into my brain and the fever into my bones, and I begin to burn and welter in my misery, I run away here. This outlook across the fields soothes me, calms me, heals me, and I am myself again." I understand. I like to do my work with a window through which I can now and then look out before me. I hold that the most perfect outlook in South London is from my study window. I live within sight of our only hill, and beautiful is that hill to me. I lay down my pen and rest my eyes upon the glorious prospect. That hill helps to make one's life tolerable.

Then, I like to see the man who insists upon having *mental* outlooks. No man's life need be utterly material. Work, but always work with outlooks towards the world of thought, with windows towards the world of genius; make the work shine with the light that comes from the loftiest range of human vision. So in a higher sense still. Life is often hard; the years become more and more exacting; but it is not a prison. The sorrows are many, the strain is sometimes terrible; but oh, the prospects! the prospects! the window of life which Christ keeps open towards heaven! I rest there. I like the sound of the word. There is not a vista that looks in that direction, but I am often there. I rest already under the shadow of the tree "whose leaves are for the healing of the nations." I listen often to the murmur of "the river of the water of life." Rest you also there this morning, and let some of the aches be smoothed out of you as you rest. Listen to the murmur of the river as it wanders through fields whose green never withers, and as you listen, the beauty, the calm, the deep peace, shall pass into your face.

But now to close.

1. This prospect is ours of God's free mercy disclosed to us in Jesus Christ. This is a sweet word to end with; for the longer we live the more we get to talk of mercy. You younger people—mind, I do not blame you—believe in what you can *do;* in your force of will, in your power of determination, in your courage. *We* believe in the divine mercy.

Here you are to-day, the light of the morning in your faces; crowned with courage, girded with enthusiasm; and the sight of you is beautiful to us. "Vanity of vanities, saith the Preacher!" "Oh, dear me, no!" say you. "The pursuit of knowledge is a weariness, the search for truth is vain," say we, who have worn our heart as well as our brain into wrinkles in the search for a goal. "Oh, but you will soon hear me cry 'Eureka!'" say you. "Science walks round in an eternal circle; Nature guards her secret too well," says the man who has scorched and half blinded himself by peering too near into her face. "Oh, she will yield her secret to me," say you. "It cannot be done," said a preacher to me, who was drawing towards the end of his work. "I believed once I could lift this neighbourhood, whether it would or no, into the arms of God;" and there was the wistful look of the beaten man in his face. "Let our turn come," say the young enthusiasts, "and the world shall see what the ministry may yet mean." "Are ye able," said our Lord to the two young men, "to drink of the cup that I shall drink of, and to be baptized with the baptism that I am baptized with?" and they—they had never tasted the bitterness of defeat—answered, "We are able." We also said it once. Grave fathers placed the work before us, and put into it its largest meanings; and we answered, "We are able." Ah, we *love* it still; it would be better to die than not to preach; but the "We are able" is never upon our lips now. *And our soul's life?* To keep the love of God burning in our hearts, to keep our hands free from stain? Oh yes, *you* can do it. *You* are standing on a rock, and the spray of temptation shall never wet *your* feet. And the dark river which divides this world from the city of the great King—*you* will cross it bravely enough, and walk up the shining stairs of the eternal city into the light, up to the feet of God. But we? Yes, we also, by "the mercy of our Lord Jesus Christ." And—

2. This is the last word: as the years move on, thought, anxiety, endeavour—everything gathers there—to make sure of that. Oh, we have had our dreams. We have been full of ambitions, we have swept all earthly prizes into our lot; but they have become infinitesimally small. I care for nothing but this—shall I attain unto the "eternal life"?

I have been on sea. I have made more than one voyage. We had some weeks before us, and we were full of plans when we started. I even proposed new subjects of study to myself which were to be pursued during the voyage. The deck of that ship presented as many industries as the streets of a great city. But one day the cry went out,

"We are getting near land." Instantly there was a great bustle of preparation. The expedients devised to while away the voyage; books with which we had been busy, half finished—everything was put away. We thought of nothing but to be ready to land. Oh, we have all of us had many projects. Realms of thought that were to be mastered, schemes of service that were to show how much could be compressed into one life lived at its best. Let us be honest. Dreams of wealth, of fame—oh yes, we have had them. But they are nothing to day; I dismiss them all. I am looking out wistfully for the shore; I want to be ready when the cry comes. Breezes from the land, laden with the fragrance of the sweet fields, are in my face. I strain my eyes. It is nigh at hand. Let me be. Perish everything, so that an "abundant entrance" be given me "into the everlasting kingdom of our Lord and Saviour Jesus Christ."

AN UNTRAMMELLED LIFE.

AN UNTRAMMELLED LIFE.

"The Lord answered me, and set me in a large place."—Ps. cxviii. 5.

THAT is a most fitting description of what the world is, of what life is to the man of God, of what the man of God's lot is. It is "a large place." Of course I understand that that is not the first meaning of the words; that that is not the idea the man had in his mind who first spoke the words. He had been in trouble; it had shut him in, had driven him into a corner. He looked round despairingly; he could not see where help could come from. There was no escape from the calamity; he was sunk in despair. But God had come in a way which was half a miracle and had opened out a road for him. The broad world was about him, hope was his once again; he had a future, and he breathed freely once more.

That is the first meaning of the words. But I want to give them to you now as a broad description of the life of the man of God, the inheritance which God has made possible for every Christian. It is a broad, rich, free, measureless life, whose whole wealth you have never counted.

I know that that is not the general conception of it. The general idea of the Christian life is, that it is a narrow, cramped life, "cribb'd, cabined, confined." The gospel is a list of prohibitions; the word oftenest upon its lips is, "Thou shalt not, thou shalt not;" you must refrain from this, you must not do that; you must not drink wine; you must deny yourself the drama; you must read nothing but the Bible—in any case nothing more secular than sermons—on Sunday. I will acknowledge that there *are* people of such curious taste that they do read the Bible, and even sermons, on Sunday, and even on other days; that there *are* people who do not drink wine, and who abstain from the noble inspirations of the English theatre. But you may believe me that they do not consider that a very great deprivation, nor do they feel that their hands are one whit tied on that ground. What I want to show you is, that the Christian is absolutely the freest and most untrammelled man in the world. Indeed, I know of no one but himself who *is* free and untrammelled. He is not penned in nor driven into a corner; he stands in a broad, open field. The horizon right round is open; north, south, east, west, life is his—his unquestioned inheritance. I am a freer man, a richer man, a blither man, a stronger man, a hopefuller man, because I am a Christian. He has "set me in a large place."

Will you let me describe my inheritance, my life, to you, as I see it to-day? And first—

I. I HAVE A GRAND, BROAD CREED. I can breathe. I count none of the things which others hold as well as I. Every one, for instance, believes in God. The Agnostic believes in God. The Positivist's one boast is that he believes in God. There is scarcely anybody who makes any pretence to be a thinker, but would consider himself insulted if you suggested that he does not believe in God.

He would resent it if you hinted that he was an atheist; would blush as if you had said that he had never been educated. It is the one thing everybody resents just now. An atheist! "Why, the only difference between you and me," says the Positivist, "is that I *spell* the word 'God' a little differently." I say, "Very well, then; I will count nothing among the special wealths of my creed which you hold as well as I." But I still contend that all the creeds are narrow compared with mine. Even those whose special pride is the breadth of their creed, who pose as "free-thinkers," are hedged in compared with me; their creed is narrow-minded side by side with mine. I say, "You live in a pit, and I live on the breezy heights; I should choke if I tried to live where you live." Listen to my creed.

1. First, a God whose love is universal; who is pledged to every soul to whom He has given being; to whom every soul is as dear as every other, and who works to realize the most perfect blessedness of all. I am never dogged with the doubt, when I stand up and look you in the face, as to whether I may dare sing the message of love in the hearing of you all, lest I should be cheating you with a song that was never meant for all.

Now, you have no hint of that anywhere but in the gospel. Nature does not teach that, if we are to believe those who will have it that they are her only competent exponents. Evolution says that Nature's method has been to crush the many to produce a superb few; to toss the million on one side and bestow all her attention upon one. I have been in an artist's studio, and I have seen there heaps of half-finished and discarded sketches. The painter would draw a hint of the idea he had in his mind; dissatisfied with it, he would toss it on one side and try again, until by-and-by he had got hold of the idea that thoroughly satisfied him, and then he would paint his picture. Nature, so says Evolution, has been doing that. She has tried a thousand experiments; always produced countless specimens before she made up her mind as to which she was going to keep, and then crumpled up all the others and ruthlessly tossed them on one side. A God who loves everything that He has made—there is no hint of Him in Nature.

History, if you read it merely from the standpoint of the scientific historian, read it in the spirit of Gibbon or Buckle, merely says, " these are the facts, these are the incidents, and this seems to be the law that determines them,"— history, I say, if you read it in that light, gives you no hint that God loves every one equally, or even that He loves the majority of men at all. The many seem to exist for the few; the multitude to live to be used by the unscrupulous souls whom history calls heroes, to serve their personal ambitions and to play their strange tricks with.

Theology has always been afraid to declare frankly and without reserve the universal love of God. Calvinism, in some shape or form, has always dogged the footsteps of the gospel. The redeemed will be "brands plucked from the burning"—a few. The many, many will be consumed—or worse, will be kept in inconceivable agony for ever and ever. We seem somehow to have been unable even to *think* a gospel without a hell in it; we have been unable to paint our radiant heaven except on the hideous background of that. Our gospel has been the song of the nightingale, sweeter somehow because the night was dark— a pathetic note sung only to those who go out in the night to seek it; and the stillness of night and the hush upon the fields have made it more pathetic. Not the song of the lark—and I hold that the song of the lark is sweeter than the song of the nightingale—which comes down from the heart of the sunlight, a rain of song poured out upon everybody. But listen! *that* is the gospel. It is sunlight, it is broad day, it is song, it is love—poured out upon everybody, offered to every one who can appreciate it. You can never be too free in the proclamation of it; you can lift up your voice with confidence; you stand in "a large place."

2. A creed which makes its best possible for everybody. The opposite of that is true of every other fact of life. In mental gifts and endowments the majority of us at best have little to boast of. The man of genius seldom comes. To-day's newspaper is crowded with names, and every other man counts himself a great man; but when the historian of fifty years hence comes to sum up our generation, he will do so in half a dozen names. The genuine schoolmaster very soon teaches himself to be content with moderate gifts in his pupils—gets to consider himself fortunate if they even rise to that level. Now and then the sculptor gets the block of marble out of which he can chisel his most perfect dream; but he has to be content with something very much less than his dream, as a rule. And so the teacher gets the youth who carries the light of the royal soul in his face now and then. He can put his best into this one; here is his grand chance of showing what he can do. But this good fortune comes very seldom. The world's special *advantages* are crowded upon the few. A splendid education, the university that can teach you how to handle your tools—reserved for the few. I have had a grudge against life right through—have always felt myself handicapped; I have never been able to do justice to

myself, to manipulate more than a segment of my soul. I was born to be something more than I have ever been able to be. The rarest souls I know at the present moment I see hedged in by circumstances. The man who has never dared to marry because he had a mother to maintain; who has denied himself the luxury of love that he might make life smooth for her; who knows what is in him to do if he had leisure; but he must work to get bread for those who are dependent upon him. The gifted woman with whom you have only to talk for five minutes and you see the aureole of genius about her head, a drudge in a village minister's home—a caged eagle. The dream you had of yourself in youth, and which under the circumstances in which you have been fixed could never be. Oh, we are not going to whine; we will be our fullest, blithest, completest possible self! But it is possible for everybody to be that into which Christ Jesus calls men; every one can be the superbest Christian; genius, wealth, circumstances, set no bound upon that. The noblest specimens of the spirit that was in Christ Jesus, of the virtues that adorned Him, I have seen in cottage homes where education had set upon the soul few of its graces; in poverty, in uncanny circumstances, in ill health; in those whose life had been handicapped from the outset. You can be a hero anywhere; you can be a saint anywhere; you may win your place in God's "legion of honour" anywhere. "Cribb'd, cabined, confined"? Nay! God has "set me in a large place."

3. Again: A creed which invites me to examine and explore it, which courts criticism, which positively invites men to do what many imagine it forbids. One of its proudest mottoes is, "I speak as unto wise men; judge ye what I say." The one favour it asks of you is that you

should test it; that you should see whether it has the right to claim to be what it professes to be; that you should take your hammer and tap every stone in the wall and see whether it be solid. It gives you absolute liberty to judge for yourself of every assertion which it makes. It sets you upon the open hills and says, "Sweep the whole horizon; go where you will; explore."

To be sure, there are some who would deny us this liberty, and who seem to be half afraid of it. We have seen kings abdicating before now; we have even read of men bartering their liberty and selling themselves into bondage. I read in the Book of Deuteronomy that the Jews had a very expressive ceremony. A man chose sometimes to be a slave when he might be free. He had served the time to which his master had a right, and was a free man again, but he preferred to remain a slave; the responsibilities of life would be fewer as a slave than as a free man, so he chose to continue in bonds. And the ceremony was this: he was brought to the door, and an awl was driven through his ear into the doorpost. Now, hosts to-day not only submit to that, but court that. They refuse to be free. They will not walk out into life and use the divine reason with which God has endowed them, and think for themselves, but they submit to priests and dogmatists and scientists, who drive an awl through their ear into the doorposts, and they go through life with the mark of the slave upon them. Only this last week the life of a once famous man—Professor Ward—has been published. Professor Ward was a Romanist—a man of beautiful life, a rare saint, a superb scholar, a consummate logician, and, within certain limits, an unerring thinker; a man who, if you once got into his grip, would throttle you and never let you go. But he handed himself and his brilliant intellect over to the Romish Church, saying, "Decide thou the limits inside which I am free to think; think thou for me." He had the awl driven through his ear into the doorpost. It is very strange. Even the Protestant often does not feel absolutely happy until his Assembly of Divines has guaranteed his faith for him, and told him exactly what to believe. He likes to have the awl driven through his ear into the doorpost.

But that is not what the *gospel* courts. The gospel invites you to explore all its territories, to dig for its hidden treasures; indeed, will only give itself to him who will question, think, search. It even coaxes you to the search. Like nature, it half hides its face with a veil to tempt you to lift it. Like the fabled goddess, it throws its golden apples before you to draw you further on. No room in the palace is locked. "Knock, and it shall be opened unto you."

Three things, then, that are axioms of my faith. A divine love which is universal, a religion whose best is possible for everybody, and absolute liberty to explore all its treasures. It "sets me in a large place."

II. A BROAD, ROUNDED, HEALTHFUL LIFE. A life that includes every sweet and noble thing.

1. Every bright and healthful pleasure. Some men's definition of the gospel is the things it prohibits. The scroll they would inscribe across the Christian temple is not, "God, who giveth us richly all things to enjoy;" but, "Touch not, taste, not, handle not." Their figure of the representative genius of the gospel would be Napoleon shut up on St. Helena, moodily coursing the heights, standing on the cliffs eating his heart out, dreaming of what he might

be, of what there is in him to do, but shut out from it all. Some people's conception of life is that everything that is pleasant, everything it is easy for the soul to love, everything which the soul covets, is forbidden. We submit because we have some vague dread of an awful doom if we dare to indulge ourselves in those things; but our souls fret and fume, and we live the poor, whining, starved life of cowards. Hear me. I was staying once with a man who possessed a noble estate. He was not a braggart, not a man who reminds you by every word he speaks of the contrast between him and you; makes you—at least, tries to make you—feel that you are poorer than you had imagined yourself to be by emphasizing the contrast between his great wealth and your slender means. There was no touch of that in my host. But we had been walking among the hills one day, and we came—with no design on his part—to a height which commanded the country for miles round. The temptation was too great even for my modest host, and he pointed out to me the distant peak and yonder river and the wood under the further hill, and said, "*That is my estate.*"

I have a great mind to point out to you what my estate in Christ Jesus is; that which this Christian life which I am trying to live is. All natural pleasures are mine. Mirth which is medicine and food is mine. All intellectual feasts are mine. Oh magic books which I love, in which I delight to dig! I have a wrestling-match with Kant or Hume sometimes. I sit down with a man like Dr. Fairbairn, and he shows me in his marvellous last volume the treasures he has been gathering for thirty years. I spend a morning at the Royal Academy, and every man has done his best to give me that aspect of nature or vision of human life which was the most beautiful that he had discovered. And I come here, and the Sunday morning is the richest and most perfect morning of the week; and sometimes, at least, the door of heaven is opened to me as it was to Stephen, and, hushed and happy, I neither argue nor prove, and I want no evidences of Christianity, but I look and see the "Son of man standing on the right hand of God." That is my estate. You who imagine that mine is a poor, cramped life, little do you know the "large place" in which God has set me.

2. A life that is to attain its blessedness, the ideal aimed at, not by prohibitions, but by growth. Gautama, the father of Buddhism, tried to sear his noblest instincts, and to kill the hunger for love and affection that was in him. Was there anything beautiful, anything which it was easy for the soul to delight in? He would deny himself that. He would put his children from him; he would tear himself from the woman whose love had once been his heaven; and, when his soul had been converted into ice, he would consider that his salvation was complete. The Christian monk's idea of salvation is to choke down every natural instinct, like thrusting a stone into the mouth of a well; to reduce life into a number of prohibitions; to suspect everything that ministers pleasure. Even the Protestant monk or nun—for there *are Protestant* monks and nuns—acts on that understanding. I remember a woman who once lived the richest, sweetest, most winning life. Children competed for a place in her affection, for a place in her Sunday school class. Christ was a sweet song in her soul. She was always the illustration that came into my mind of what was bravest and comeliest in the gospel. But the dead blight of Plymouth Brethrenism fell upon her. She had the instincts of the artist in her, and she began to suspect them, and to make a virtue of wearing dresses designed by the genius

of ugliness. Literature had been food to her once, but she swept from her the choicest little library; the poets and the scientists became banished books. She was an admirable musician, but Beethoven became a heathen to her, and she was never absolutely happy except when she was strumming Sankey's hymns. She starved herself—God help her!— starved herself to please the God who had made her a comely woman, and inspired Beethoven, and created the soul of Shakespeare, and put the painter's brush in Turner's hand. Poor woman! she defrauded herself. The way to kill the bad life in you—"the old man," as Paul calls it— is not by clipping this, that, and the other, but by filling yourself with the rich graces of life as seen in Christ Jesus. Courage and sweet help for those who need it, the brave love that can bear any cross—the life of Jesus,—there is room in that; it is "a large place." Live it, and you will grow into God's own bliss.

III. THE NOBLEST ENTERPRISES, THE MOST ROYAL WORK, THE GRANDEST AIMS, FOR THE BETTERMENT OF THE WORLD.

1. John banished to Patmos sat on a rock, and, looking out over the sea, forgot himself in a dream. When we are weary, and hope is dying in us, we still turn to that dream. But I also have had my dream, and I will tell it to you. First, our grand missionary hopes have been realized. The behest which we have obeyed is, "Go ye into all the world, and preach the gospel to every creature;" the word which has cheered us is, "And I, if I be lifted up, will draw all men unto Me," and, "The kingdoms of this world *are* become the kingdoms of our Lord and His Christ." Then look! War has been abolished; the nations of Europe are no longer armed to the teeth; peace—I do not mean "armed neutrality," two emperors meeting to exchange courtesies,

and all Europe wondering which shall fly first at the other's throat;—but genuine peace, grounded in brotherly love and confidence, knits all nations together. Labour wars have become impossible; men read the story of them just as we now examine a cannon-ball dug up in an old battle-field, and refer to them only as proofs of the barbarism of the past. Christian brotherhood welds the Churches, and there is no rivalry but the rivalry as to which shall render the world the largest service. Education has ceased to mean catechisms and schoolmasters who have the hearts of priests. The London County Council has been recognized as a Christian institution. There is no drunkenness; no Englishman who would not be ashamed to ask for a licence to poison his brother. Every music-hall in London has been purified; the mouths of singers have been sweetened, and every vile purlieu of hell has been closed. Music discourses sweet sounds in every park in London, and opens some window of heaven to the haggard and toilworn. The picture-gallery is everywhere, and open every day of the week, and we have ceased to spite those who will not join us in public worship by saying that they shall not refresh themselves with the sweet ministries of art. The shop-hand is no longer overworked; the seamstress has a soul fresh enough on Sunday to catch some glimpse of the inheritance which in Christ Jesus is hers also.

Such is my dream; and when the gospel gets to be understood, when England has become indeed a Christian country, every one will see that all those things flow naturally from the gospel, that the gospel fully translated means all those things. I have wandered through the villages of Lower Egypt, roamed through its fields and sauntered through its gardens. The streams are everywhere, and the country, bursting with fertility, is laden with corn; and I understand how, in the grim desert of Horeb, Israel sighed for "the cucumbers, and the melons, and the leeks, and the onions, and the garlic." The country asks for nothing but water; give it that, and it becomes a veritable Eden. But I have gone a little further south, and stood on the bridge at Cairo, and found that every brooklet is but a branch of the one great river. And so, I delight in all the streams that irrigate human life—peace, and brotherly love, and philanthropy, and pure education; but as I follow them up to their birth, I find that they are only branchlets of the broad river of God, the river that floweth from under "the throne of God and the Lamb."

2. And now, to work for the realization of this dream broadens a man, broadens him as nothing else does. A man may have a broad creed whilst he is the smallest of all small souls; may be loud in his boast of being a "freethinker" and be as narrow-minded as a man can be. What calls itself culture is often only another name for selfishness and littleness. The character depicted in "Robert Elsmere"—the university don, who had won all honours, but who was too proud to embody what he knew in any bit of solid work, lest there should be some flaw in the work which somebody might be able to criticize—was that of a cultured man, but his was a small, shrunken soul, in whom even love and manliness gradually died. Positivism, which, as Comte first saw it, was to organize itself into a missionary society to evangelize the heathen, and to set up the kingdom of God in Africa, and to show there what a redeemed humanity meant, has been sitting from that day to this gazing upon the beautiful air-castle which it had conjured into existence, lecturing about it, and proving that

it is *not* an air-castle. It has *done* nothing; its first missionary has not gone out to Africa yet; and Comte's representatives in England meet every Sunday to contend that wisdom dwells with them, and that if the world were wise it would join them in the worship of their air-castle, and in talking, I suppose, about setting up the kingdom of God in Africa. It may be audacious to say so, but nothing is to be seen on the face of the earth this morning to which the world owes so little, nothing so calculated to blight the soul that makes it its creed.

Broaden the soul! Nothing broadens the soul like work for the wants and woes of men, and nothing inspires men to work like the dreams, the hopes, and promises of the gospel of Jesus Christ. We have caught a vision of the world as *He* saw it, yearned for it, died for it. We also carry this world in our heart; the African, the Hindoo, the South Sea Islander, are also children of God, and we will toil for their redemption. Our hearts go out to all men. We stand in no cramped or narrow room, but in "a large place."

IV. AND NOW, LASTLY: I HAVE NOBLE AND INSPIRING HOPES. Rich indeed are the hopes which the gospel gives me; immortality is a grand word. I find "a large place" for myself under the broad skies of "eternal life."

Man, according to the gospel, has room to grow and time to grow. Over-hurry spoils the best work. The author publishes his book with an apology; he fondly believes that with a little leisure he might have made it a work worth reading; he sends it out with many misgivings, but he must send it as it is or never give it to the world. The noblest picture, grandly conceived, is spoiled because the painter was overdriven. The marks of haste are upon it; it is an unfinished work. I have given up a study which had got to mean much to me—given it up with keen regret. I had got hold of the subject, it was beginning to reveal its wealth to me, but the crowded calls of daily duty compelled me to let it go. My books reproach me still as I look at them. We hurry through a subject, feeling that we must have a taste of it; we take a hurried draught, though we know that we can never drink deep of it. Few of us have the courage of Browning's Grammarian, who refused to hurry; who never dreamt that he could finish his studies here, but was sure that he should be allowed to finish them yonder. Let us also be a little wiser; we will not get scared and spoil our work by over-hurry. Eternity is ours. Within four hundred yards of this spot, in an old garden, are two trees. Both of the same species, planted on the same day. One in a close corner. It is shrunken and, I was going to say, peevish; for there *are* peevish *trees*. The other in the centre of the garden. It has grown to be its largest self; a right royal tree, an ornament to its surroundings. It grows in " a large place." So I have many objections to the substitutes proposed for the gospel—Materialism, Positivism, and many others—and this if I had no other objection—they propose to plant me in a corner. Give me room; plant me with the noble sky of immortality over me; I will grow into my full stature then. Set me where God set me—in " a large place."

PROPHETS AND SONS OF THE PROPHETS.

PROPHETS AND SONS OF THE PROPHETS.

"Ye are the sons of the prophets."—Acts iii. 25.

THEREFORE whatsoever the prophets did you may do. God is as near to you as He ever was to them. He may inspire you for the work of the hour—to understand its problems and to fight its battles, just as He inspired them for the problems and battles of their day. God did not speak to men for the last time nineteen hundred years ago. You may refuse to listen; you may lose yourself in the clatter of talk about physical science and business and a dead world in which there is no sign of God left, and you may never hear His voice. But He *is* speaking, and it is only your fault that you miss that voice.

Mr. Leslie Stephen—the most miserable comforter of the hour—spoke in his usual depressing strain the other evening. The age of Shakespeare and Milton is over, so he said. We can never have another Chaucer. Science, even, in the romantic sense in which Bacon was a scientist, is impossible. There can never be a great theologian again; never another Augustine or Calvin. The world has become stale, dull, prosy; its romance is over. We can do no more than expound and annotate and publish new versions of Shakespeare, or Calvin's "Theological Institutes," with expansions and footnotes. Others expatiate on the sad fact—at least, they say it is a fact—that *Art* has become impossible. Art died in the Middle Ages. Art, in any case, must find its *subjects* in the past. Life was picturesque and romantic three hundred or a thousand years ago, and if you want subjects, you must paint Madonnas or revive the legends of old Greek mythology. Others protest that the steam-engine has wiped out the last line of picturesqueness left in English life; John Ruskin says so still. But Turner, in his famous picture of the steam-engine rushing at fullest speed, produced one of the most poetic pictures ever painted—as poetic and picturesque as the same painter's old battle-ship, the *Temeraire*. The poetry, the romance, the pathos, is here, if you have the eye to see it. Poetry was not buried in Tennyson's grave, and, given the "eye to see," we may have Raphaels and Murillos yet, who shall find their subjects in the romance of these commonplace days. Romance! Ay, life still *teems* with romance.

And so here. We may be sons not only of the scientists and poets, of the critics and painters; we may be "sons of the prophets;" we may receive messages as direct as any message they ever received, and do work as distinctly divine as they ever did.

That, then, is my subject—the prophet, the prophet of the present hour, of *to-day*.

1. ENGLAND AS WELL AS JUDÆA HAS HAD ITS PROPHETS; and it is of the English prophet I want to speak. The prophet has always been the same man, whether in England or in Judæa. The form which his work has taken may be different in England from what it was in Judæa,

but it has been essentially the same work. And, to start with—

1. The prophet is, first of all, the *good* man; the witness for truth and righteousness; the witness, not by his genius, not by the work he is able to do, but by what he *is*. That in the Old Testament, is always the sign that a man is a genuine prophet—his soul burnt with a passion for goodness, for purity, for religion. The prophet would sometimes be a herdsman, sometimes a statesman; sometimes what we to-day would call an orator, a gifted speaker; sometimes a man of the plainest speech, who hesitated, stuttered and stammered—a man to whom to deliver an oration would be the one impossible task; sometimes a layman, a courtier like Daniel; sometimes like Ezekiel, a priest; but he was always a noble *man*.

You have noticed that in the Old Testament story there were "schools of the prophets," what we to-day would call theological colleges; but it did not follow that because a man had had a theological education he was a prophet, any more than it follows to-day that because a man has a college imprimatur upon him, God ever intended him to stand up in His name. The prophet, who cut himself into the conscience of his generation, who fired its enthusiasm, never or seldom had the mark of any school upon him. Elijah and Amos belonged to no school. And even if a man did belong to a school, the first thing he had to do before he became a prophet who told upon his day, was to wipe out from himself every sign of his school.

To-day there are "schools" of *art*, but every one who has been trained in the school is not an *artist*. The first thing the artist has often to do is to emancipate his own soul, and shake off every sign of the school. The coveted

"R.A." is often simply the sign that a man has not emancipated himself from the trammels of his school—the certificate given to the prosy soul who has never risen above rules. There are "schools" of *music*. If a man have the soul of music in him, the school may do him good; but the school cannot make him a musician. If there be no music *in* him, the only thing the school will probably confer upon him will be conceit and affectation. So there were "schools of the prophets," which turned out a prophet now and then, but turned out many who were not prophets. They had gone through all the drill, were perfect masters of the technicalities of their calling; they had a high sense, I have no doubt, of what was due to their order, of the respect that ought to be paid to them; but the fire that burns in the prophet's soul—the passion for truth, for goodness, for purity, the courage that would fight any battle for God—*that* burnt but feebly in them. *They* were no prophets.

The prophet before everything was a good man, consumed with a passion for righteousness.

2. Then, secondly, the prophet was the man moved by what he saw and felt to *act*; to whom to *do* was the first necessity. Not only a man who understood the times, but who rose up to do the things which the times demanded; who not only saw, but who dared not be silent. Elijah the Tishbite was not the only man in Israel who saw the curse that Ahab was to the land. There were "seven thousand," so we read, "who had not bowed the knee to Baal;" but he was the only man who dared to confront the man who had really troubled Israel. To remain in his solitude, brooding over the curse that had come upon the country, was impossible to him. He bearded the king, and in

burning words foretold the doom that was coming. That man was the prophet.

Three things in this respect make the prophet, and the man is never a prophet unless the three be in him.

First, He has the "eye to *see*." Nothing tortures you more than a man who tries to console you, but does not understand you; who imagines he is soothing you, when every word he utters cuts your soul until it bleeds. How many good people you have known who have been a terror to you! They did not mean it, but every word of theirs rasped you. They wanted to help, but they did not know where the problems of life hurt you—good, tender-hearted souls, brimming over with concern and sympathy; but your soul shut itself up, and you could die rather than talk of your difficulties to them. Others read you at their first glance; their first word proves that they have plumbed your soul's deepest depths. Like the physician who has the "eye to see," they lay their finger upon your soul and say, "Thou ailest here, and here." Like Daniel, who found the king agitated with his dream—it haunted him, though it had vanished from his mind—and said, "This was what the king saw, this was the dream," and the excited king cried, "That *was* the dream." Carlyle was such a man. "Sartor Resartus" was the cry of an age; the world was ailing, was sick unto death from mental sorrows which he—grim soul—described. Coleridge was another. Coleridge set his finger exactly upon the weak point in English theology; showed exactly why the theology of the hour had become empty husk which could be bread for nobody. Matthew Arnold—I mean the poet, and not the critic—was another. Matthew Arnold's sonnets—some of them—are the sobs of an England that wanted to believe and could not. These three men read their fellows; there was one line of the prophet's gift in every one of them, but not one of them was a prophet. They knew the ailment, but could not heal it; they diagnosed the fever, but could not allay it. That first—the prophet reads his age, the prophet sees.

Then, secondly, the prophet *feels*. What he sees moves him, haunts him, draws a veil of sadness over his face. Many who imagine they are sitting at the feet of Jesus are calmly indifferent to the sorrows and woes of the world. What do hosts who "sit down to the feast" in our churches every Sunday care for the heathen London over which you fret? The grimmest problems of the hour never worry them; the wail of overworked men and the tasks that dishearten the Church never rob them of an hour's peace. The philanthropist may rack his brain to devise some means by which he may fight the public-house and stem the black flood of heathenism which, in spite of everything, is creeping up. But the grim social questions that torture you—the problem of poverty, the bitter war between the moneyed and unmoneyed class—before which you stand beaten and bewildered, never flutter many into a moment's anxiety. Others there are to whom everything that pertains to man is, to be sure, a matter of interest, but the interest is purely intellectual; who are ready to note everything, to classify everything; who find in every fact that crops up, as the story of the world unfolds, some illustration of what they consider the beneficent and beautiful law of evolution. Gibbon affected this—affected to be an absolutely impartial observer, a chronicler of history pure and simple. The thing that concerned him most was that he had found a subject that exactly fitted his special genius, and gave him the material out of which to work out an immortal book. The most popular French novelist of the hour seems to imagine that he has marked out for himself a noble line of work in leading those whom he can persuade to accompany him through the vilest moral sewers. He is a student of humanity, forsooth, and every one shall see under his guidance the bog in which society is sinking. He never sheds a tear, his voice never quivers: pity is no concern of the artist's—let him *describe*. The preacher, even, may be too ready to imagine that he has done everything when he has merely done that—merely analyzed and expounded his text; set it in the crucible, and shown exactly what it contains. But let him not deceive himself; he has not preached until he has melted his own soul. "Eloquence is logic set on fire;" and the preacher no more than the historian, the novelist, or the poet, is a prophet unless he be moved. Ay, *moved*. The prophet is the moved man, the man who has made the sorrows and problems of his generation his own; the throes of his hour beat in him. Every shock of the French Revolution broke through Carlyle's heart. Carlyle was not a spectator, but he tasted the bliss and the horrors of it. Carlyle in this also was a prophet. The hand of Tennyson was on the religious pulse of England for fifty years; he felt the fever that burnt in us, and always sang in clear notes what we were trying to say. We will gratefully set him also "among the prophets."

Once again: The prophet descries the remedy. He is the "seer." But even that is not all. He is not "prophet" merely because he is "seer." The prophet embodies his vision—works out what he sees. One of you has often talked to me about General Booth; about his emigration schemes, his farm colonies, and wonderful philanthropic work. You have insisted again and again, and you are right, that the idea did not originate with the Salvation Army leader. You know how I admire the man; taking him all in all, we shall not soon see his like again. But the idea was born in another man's brain; a man known to but very few; a man as unpractical as he is original and daring in his schemes. It seethed and simmered in this man's brain, oozed out in enchanting talk whenever he could get a sympathetic listener. But the redoubtable Salvationist gets the idea—gets it from this very man —and it is translated into work in six months. Not a dream, not talk, was it with him, but *work*. That is the prophet. The *other* man is a seer; this man is a *prophet*.

3. The prophets are of many orders. I will mention a few.

The great preachers. That goes without saying. England has had a noble line of them. "Apostolic succession" is a silly fiction, but it is also a superb fact. Every new era in religion has been created by the preacher. New theology is a dead letter until the tongue of the preacher has caught it. The great theologian may move the few, but it is the preacher that moves the many. It was Luther and not Erasmus that moved Europe, that created the Reformation. Luther was not a theologian, but a preacher. It was John Wesley and Whitefield, and not Bishop Butler, that shook England from its slumber. It was Frederick Robertson of Brighton, and not Dr. McLeod Campbell, that killed the pagan theory of the Atonement. It was Charles Haddon Spurgeon, and not Dr. Hodge, that kept the candle of Puritan theology burning up to yesterday. It was Henry Ward Beecher, the preacher, that took the sting out of the theory of evolution. "It demolishes the

Bible," the unbelievers said. "Why, the Bible is a truer book than ever," men got to feel as they listened to the preacher. "Nothing has done more to ensure the immortality of the Bible than the theory of evolution," said Beecher. Revelation has grown like a tree; the Bible becomes a greater book from page to page. Revelation is like the seed of corn: "first the blade, then the ear, then the full corn in the ear." No! No truth is established until it comes into the pulpit; the man who sets the hall-mark upon it and gives it currency is always the preacher.

The great poets; and England has had a grand succession of them. We are only slowly getting to understand the poet's mission. The poet is not the mere reciter of the deeds of the past, the mere romancist or troubadour, though we do not despise *him*. The world will never grow weary of Homer. The tale of the past can never be told by the mere historian; we never understand the past until the poet has told it—until, in any case, the historian who has the soul of the poet in him has told it. Neither is the poet the mere exponent of the mirth and hope and delight in life which bubble up in all men in their brightest moments, though he is *that;* not the mere dispeller of our dark thoughts and dyspepsia, though he is *that*. Shakespeare has brightened hosts in every generation for three hundred years; broken the clouds of their despair and moodiness. Spring breaks wherever he comes; his harp is always in perfect tune, and the air becomes fresh, and demons flee at his first note. But the poet is more than that. The poet always catches first the light that is beginning to break upon the mystery that has got to haunt us, is always the first to descry the dawn. It is he always opens the prison-doors against which we are beating our souls. The theologian, the scientist, the politician, only come *after* the poet. The House of Commons is now only slowly translating the Corn Law Rhymes into legislation. Darwin simply caught and amplified the dream which Lucretius saw; and the glowing visions in which we rejoice, of a broader gospel and a "larger hope," are merely the "new heavens and a new earth" of which Browning had long sung.

The great reformers—creators of new eras. And these are always the world's great saints. Froude has just been stirring Oxford into great excitement with his talks about the British navy. England is continually boasting of its navy; an Englishman never so absolutely looks down upon all the world as he does when he begins to talk of the English navy. And Froude, in discussing the Tudor period—and if there is one era of English history which he knows, it is that—has just been telling the university—to the horror and dismay of many, I have no doubt—that the English navy was created by the Puritans. It is very easy to caricature and gibbet these men. They laid themselves open to criticism which is perfectly just in many respects. Their theology, much of it, was ugly enough; they never quite understood what religious liberty meant. Do not let us blink facts, the Puritans knew the way to persecute, and did persecute. But the Puritan lived as under the eye of God. If there was one thing that he was sure of, it was God; God was as real to him as the man whose hand he gripped and into whose face he looked. These men were prophets, and these men were England's heroes. It was they who created the English navy, demolished the Spanish Armada, struck the last blow which settled for ever that England was to be free. I thank Froude for that bit of English history.

In any case, Puritanism crushed the last attempt made by a British sovereign to be a tyrant. Tyranny was buried in the grave of Charles. And the men that did it— Cromwell, Milton, Pym—did no hard things? Nay, we cannot say that; stern times demand stern deeds, stern weapons. But these men were made out of the stuff of which prophets are made. And now—

II. YOU ARE IN THE SUCCESSION OF THESE PROPHETS. "Ye are the *sons* of the prophets."

1. That is your incalculable advantage. There are truths which the prophets have established that will never need to be opened up again. That is a great gain. The law of gravitation has been settled for ever. We shall not need to discuss that again. Columbus proved once for all that the earth was a sphere; the mariner may calculate upon that—may make ready for his voyage and feel sure that he will not be called upon to reconsider that. So there are social, political, and religious battles that will never have to be fought again. We shall never need another Magna Charta; the woes of the seventeenth century will never repeat themselves; no one will attempt to pass another Act of Uniformity; the universities have opened their doors to all comers, and a man will never again be tempted to tamper with his conscience in order to secure their most coveted privileges. Those battles, once won, will never have to be fought again. So also of the great questions of theology. The hideous doctrines which tortured our fathers, once swept out of the Church, will never re-invade it. The nightmare of Calvinism will scare none of us any more. We shall never need again to apologize for the Cross because we imagine it was intended to pacify the wrath of an angry God. The election which meant a limit

set upon the redemptive purposes of the Father of all, and which haunted the souls of the timid, will never be preached again. The light of hope for all men, the love of God bent upon the salvation of all men—*that* is the gospel we have received from our fathers; received from the prophets; received from McLeod Campbell and Robertson, from Samuel Cox and Beecher, from Maurice and Thomas Lynch, and many more.

And now you stand upon the threshold of life—" sons of the prophets." What will you make of it? Solomon, when he came to build the temple, found all but everything ready to his hand. David had made great preparation, for the house was to be " exceeding magnificent;" " cedar-wood " and " wrought stones " in great store had been laid up. It was for Solomon to see that the temple should be worthy of the preparation that had been made for it. So you, who are just stepping out into life. The generations that have preceded you—I will venture to say, *the generation that has immediately preceded you*—has been hard at work; but we sometimes feel that we have been doing nothing but preparing material, *making ready for* you. Scholars, theologians, preachers even, " hewing wrought stones " and cutting cedars; digging in these Scripture quarries, and making sure what it is that the divine book says. And now it is for you to *build*. It is for *you* to determine the design into which the temple is to grow, the pattern into which its pillars are to be hewn, the forms in which Christian enthusiasm shall express itself. Will you remember this?—" *Ye are the sons of the prophets.*"

2. It is more than an advantage—it is an inspiration. I have read a book written by a famous English soldier, who bears an honoured name—the son of one of the greatest

theologians the English Church ever produced. One chapter describes the course of study which every young English soldier ought to set to himself, and one item is this: he should read the life of every great English soldier, immerse himself in the study, catch the spirit of the heroes, discover the secret of their genius. I know a man at the present moment whom I revere—a noble specimen of an English man of business. I have often found him busy studying the story of his own family, tracing the line back through father, grandfather, great-grandfather—honourable men of business every one of them. And when I have come upon him so engaged, he has said, "I often go over the story of my forefathers' lives; I remind myself of what they were, for I must live to be worthy of them." Young men and women, ministers' children many of you, listen. I remind you of the homes in which you were nurtured. I remind you of what your fathers were, of the lives they lived, of their abandonment to every call of God that came to them. I recall for you the early morning worship. *You were the wee one, perhaps, who tottered with the family Bible to the table.* You remember it all—the tones of your father's voice are in your ears now; the hush of that holy season; the pleadings of the strong "man of God," "the saint, the father, and the husband;" your eyes become dim as you remember. I would not dishonour his memory, if I were you. I would not be a rake, or an idler, or a spendthrift; I would be a *man*. I would not be frivolous, or shallow-souled and empty-headed, if I were you; I would be a godly *woman*. "Ye are the sons" and daughters "of the prophets."

3. Once again: That you inherit these memories is a great responsibility. Last week died a well-known and

honoured nobleman—the Earl of Carnarvon. He bore the name worthily, for he *was* indeed a *noble* man. No man was ever perhaps less understood; but he was a man burdened with a sense of what England had the right to expect from him, because he was noble born. His responsibility was for him a heavy load. I honour this man's name; I revere his memory. Indignation has often filled us as we have watched men of his order, and asked, Is *this* the stuff out of which "noblemen" are made?

But listen! Will *you* forget who *you* are? You are *Englishmen:* the blood of Shakespeare, Milton, Bacon, is in you. You are *Protestants:* the hand of Cranmer, Ridley, Latimer, John Rogers, is upon you. You are *Puritans:* Greenwood, Barrow, Penry, were your forefathers. That is the succession in which you stand. Shall your lives be small, narrow, wicked, mean? I leave you with one sentence: "Ye are the sons of the prophets."

FAITH FOUND IN UNEXPECTED PLACES.

FAITH FOUND IN UNEXPECTED PLACES.

"Verily I say unto you, I have not found so great faith, no, not in Israel."—MATT. viii. 10.

FAITH—religious faith, the most genuine faith—is found in the most unexpected places. It may surprise you; but if you are wise, you will hail, welcome, cherish, and make much of it. You get excited when you discover a flower at the foot of the glacier or growing out of the face of the rock; it proves how indigenous to the earth the flower is. And you read Plutarch's "Lives" of the noble heathen, the great pagan saints, the moral heroes whom he loved to delineate; or you read Farrar's "Seekers after God"—the three noble men, heathen saints who lived up to the truth they knew as none of us do to the truths we know, and whose faces were always wistfully turned towards heaven, to seek more light. If you have real courage in you, and refuse to allow the dogmas of theology to choke your heart, you will see what it means—that God finds His way to souls outside the pale of the gospel. And you will be glad of it; it will be a relief to you to feel that the huge mass of the human race whom we have not yet enlightened and won

—of course, we will always toil for that—but in the mean while we will rejoice that it is not one sodden mass of ignorance and iniquity. Men's faith, men's love of the good they know, will strike you, will sometimes fill you with a sense of shame as you remember what Christendom is, what the life of the Church is. "I have not found so great faith, no, not in Israel."

But that is not what I want exactly to speak about this morning. "Faith" has a much stronger hold of man than he imagines. Those whose one pride it is—and they constantly boast of it—that they allow "faith" to determine nothing for them, show much more remarkable faith, a faith more absolute and complete than the faith of those whom they look down upon with a kind of intellectual contempt. If you want illustrations of what an absolute creature of faith man is, I would not go to find them in the Christian, in the man who has made the Bible the basis of his hope. The faith of the Christian is as nothing compared with the faith of the man whose one boast it is that in nothing does he rely upon faith, that he is absolutely independent of it. My illustrations of the hold faith has upon man are the Materialist, the Agnostic, the Positivist. There was more faith in Mr. Frederic Harrison's last New Year's Address than in every sermon I have preached for twelve months put together. I read and lifted up my hands in wonder; "I had not found such great faith, no, not in Israel." If I want to find proofs of how indigenous faith is to the soul of man, I look not to the Church, but outside the Church, to those who are often the most determined opponents of the Church.

I say two things, then.

I. THE FAITH OF THOSE WHO REJECT THE GOSPEL IS MORE REMARKABLE EVEN THAN THE FAITH OF THOSE WHO RECEIVE IT. I candidly confess that in the domain of religion I exercise faith, and I make no apology for it. I exercise my faith just as I exercise my imagination, my thinking faculty, or any small power of putting an argument which I may possess. I believe in my "faith" faculty as much as I believe in one of them. I no more dream of making an apology for my faith than Tennyson would have dreamt of apologizing for the imagination which created his "Princess" or his "Idylls of the King." I am proud of my "faith" and the feats it accomplishes, but I contend—I was going to say that I apologize—that my opponent who contemptuously smiles upon my "faith" exercises *much* "*greater* faith" than I.

Think of that for a moment. Let me give you a few items of my creed.

1. God. I think of the books that have made the deepest impression upon my mind, that have taught me to think, that have given me the noblest conceptions as to what I should endeavour to carve my life into. I never dream that I am proving myself to be an intellectual simpleton because I talk of the *authors* of those books. Every one of them was born in the brain of some one who felt himself compelled to deliver his message—born in throes and agonies sometimes. I never make an apology because I am so simple-minded as to imagine that there must be an author for every book.

I listen to a superb piece of music. The man who sits at the piano well translates it. It thrills *him*, it stirs up the deepest emotions in *me*. My soul lives in every instinct; I think, I dream, I create new worlds, and the problems that have haunted me become clear whilst the hand of the musician is upon me. I never imagine that I have proved myself a dotard because I ask, "Who wrote this music?" for, I say, he must have sometimes rocked under the same winds that have swept my soul.

I wander under the shadows of a great cathedral. A holy hush which I call worship falls upon me. The great men have been those to whom those who knew and revered them have given a resting-place here. Their greatness was that they served the world. One of the first questions I ask is, "Who designed this church? who built it?" The architect was a poet and a saint in the days in which this church was built. But the mould in which great architects' souls were run seems somehow to have been broken up; nobody now seems to have the genius that can design a church; every modern church which makes any pretence to architecture is either ugly or uncomfortable, or both. But there were souls who knew the secret once, and I never blush because I ask who designed or built this.

So, I add, here is the wonderful universe in the midst of which I find myself placed; the majesty of it is sometimes awful; the sublimity, sometimes the pathos of it, overpowering. It is an enchanting poem, an inspiring anthem, a holy temple where it is easy to worship. I can no more imagine this without God, than I can imagine that the holy Book under my hand came into existence and no one wrote it; that this church piled itself up stone by stone and that no one planned it; that the anthem which stirred our hearts a few moments ago never once boiled for the first time out of the soul of the man to whom it came as a command and a vision, saying, "Speak the thing which thou hast seen to others." *But*, will you please observe, I can give no absolute proof of this.

People used, I know, to write what were called *proofs* of the existence of God. Paley did. Paley's argument from design was once a famous one. Dr. Clarke did. His great argument was a superb piece of thinking; but let us frankly acknowledge he never *proved* the existence of God. The famous argument is not complete. There *is* no argument which cannot be controverted. The author of the Epistle to the Hebrews, whoever he was, never pretended that he had *proved* the existence of God. "By *faith*," said he, "we understand that the worlds have been framed by the word of God." Dr. Clarke's proof and Paley's proof are perfect as far as they go. Perfect chains; there is not one weak link in either of them; but the last link which binds the chain to God is not an argument, not a proof, but *faith*. "Great faith!" you say, and so it is. But this faith is nothing to the faith of those who controvert us. The account they give of the origin of the world shows wonderfully "*greater* faith." There never was such faith as that of those who pride themselves that they believe nothing which cannot be proved, demonstrated. Poor and weak indeed is our faith compared with theirs.

For listen how they account for everything that is. "Nobody made anything or called anything into existence," says one. "Nobody lighted the fire, the fire lighted itself; 'spontaneous combustion' accounts for everything. Universal death reigned once, but universal death burst into life, and you have this universe, exhaustless in its wonders." "There was no need for any one to make anything," says another. "There was no need to light the fire. There is nothing now which has not always been. Good and bad are two sides of the same thing. There is no difference between the murderer at the bar and the judge who tries him; both are God in two different moods." "God is only a handy *name*," says a third. "The universe is well able to look after itself, and requires nobody to look after it. It is a good thing to have a grand name for our noblest conceptions of virtue and self-denial, and the perfect mastery of ourselves, and we will call it God, and sing hymns to it and worship it." The Positivist, the Pantheist, the Materialist, are perhaps better men than I—I dare not boast; and in *faith* they even surpass and shame me. A universe created by Almighty God, the God of love, requires faith; but a universe which started of its own accord, a universe in which vice is as good as virtue, in which there is no moral difference between them, any more than there is a difference between black and blue, requires more faith. My faith is nothing to that. "I have not found *so great faith*, no, not in Israel."

2. Take, next, the wondrous story of our redemption as given in the gospel. There are scenes in that story which are hard to make credible. There are doctrines here which it is the most difficult thing in the world to put into a clear, consistent, and reasonable form. One of the most brilliant theologians of the hour has just made a fresh attempt to restate the doctrine of the Trinity. The keenest thinkers have been busy in every age trying to state that doctrine, but no statement which has ever been made has satisfied everybody. There are no half a dozen of you who would state it in exactly the same form. I frankly say, to accept the Trinity requires "great faith." But take the simple gospel story, take the pith of it, and never mind theology for a moment. Let me tell the story.

This human being, however he came to be what he is, is bound by indelible ties to God. The ape may have been his forefather, if you like, but some day a fire began burning in him which set him in "his own place," and made him other than an ape. Adam was a *man* and not an ape, and between the two is a great gulf. There is no measure to man's worth in the sight of God. Often of vulgar instincts and saturated in unholy lusts, God yet carries him in His heart; he has forgotten from whom he came, but nevertheless God has not put him from His thoughts. Our Lord Jesus Christ is God come to seek man: not a messenger from God, but *God*. Miracles dropped from His hands; they were the pity of God for the hungry, for the sorrowful, for the sin-laden, for the sad. God has set it to Himself to win man, and *must* win him; to Him man is a personal necessity. Desperate was the strait in which man was set. I do not know that we can tell exactly and literally what it was, but no one could save man who declined to taste death, and in Christ the wave of death passed over the head of God. We, with our wretched reading of death as meaning ceasing to be, have shrunk from saying this. But when I die I shall not cease to be, and God *did* bow His head under the wave, and He carried man through with Him.

It is an exquisite story; it thrills you, it breaks men down even when they cannot believe it. The genius of it, the daring of it—it is marvellous; the superbest idyl the world has ever heard, the Divine romance. I have sometimes been afraid to believe in it. There is *too much* of God in it; it cannot be; let us frankly acknowledge it does require "great faith" to absolutely believe it.

But I will tell you a story which requires greater faith.

God made me and forgot me, made me and ceased to care for me, made me and put me out of His thoughts, made me and had not one wistful longing after me, lost me and did not feel bereaved, lost me and never missed me.

A controversy has been going on in the newspapers with regard to the great steamer which was disabled the other day in mid-Atlantic. Scornful things have been said, because, as usual, we have been in an over-hurry. Two steamers have been accused of abandoning this sister-steamer to the mercy of a pitiless sea. One was said to have cut the ropes by which the disabled steamer was bound to it, and escaped like a mean coward. No wonder that the man accused should have demanded the right to speak. Had he done that, the scorn of every seaman would have hounded him from the sea. But that is what men say *God* has done. Father, forgive us, that we have so maligned Thee! God took me out into the ocean of life; the storms have broken upon me, sin has disabled me and I am sinking, and God has cut the ropes and left me. Worship that God! Had he been that, it would have been *base* to worship Him. Believe that? Believe it who can, and if there be any man who believes it, I can only say, "I have not seen such great faith, no, not in Israel."

3. Think of one grave question more. What awaits man when this life is over? What shall we say death is? A door into a larger and more perfect life, say we. Extinction, say those who controvert our contention; life has burnt itself out like a candle into its socket, and can never be rekindled again.

Now, to believe that life continues, that this life is the prelude to a more perfect life, that death is the natural order by which man rises to a higher life, the bursting of the bud, the blossom breaking into flower, the sunset which implies a glorious sunrise,—to believe this helps one, girds one with strength, makes one brave to do and to endure; and this is a certainty to faith, but to nothing else but faith.

Let me say at once there is no absolute proof of immortality unless you accept the proof you have in Jesus Christ, and even the proof you have in Him is only a proof to faith. Oh, I know all the arguments. I remember Cicero's; I remember the logic of it, here and there the wistful pathos of it; it is a grand argument, Cicero's immortal monument. I know the argument from evolution; for you must understand that there are Christian evolutionists —evolutionists who use their grand theory to establish the contention of the gospel as well as evolutionists who use it to destroy that contention. The great American evolutionist, Dr. Asa Grey, the Darwin of the United States, as I might call him, contends that immortality is a necessary inference from evolution; that man, having come so far from the monad, the mollusc, the ape, cannot stop here —he must mount higher. The argument is well put, but it is no *proof*. I know the poet's argument. I know the argument of "In Memoriam"—the grand protest against death. I have read Tennyson's letters; I know that he felt more intensely, perhaps, on this than on any other subject. He protested against God if there was to be no life for man beyond death. "I would beard Him," said he, "and tell Him that He had betrayed me: life there *must* be." I go one step further still; I leave Cicero's logic, the evolutionist's inference based on cold science, the poet's pathetic *claim* to continue to live, and I go to the grave of Jesus and find there still greater certainty. But every inference I make is only a proof to faith; it is no *demonstration* of life beyond death. That life is only a certainty to me "by faith." Great is the Christian's faith.

But I will show you far "greater faith" than that; all such faith pales into insignificance compared with the faith of the man who denies for himself a future life. It requires faith to believe that that life is a certainty, but it is nothing compared with the faith that can believe that there is no such life. For listen! I have known a man spend patient years gathering materials for a book; the great idea that he proposed to embody in the book had dwelt with him, grown upon and become grander to him the longer he had lived with it, and when the material was ready he burnt it. I have seen the painter work hard to embody his dream, to make the vision which had dwelt in the sanctuary of his imagination visible in his picture, and then tear his knife through the picture and destroy it. I have known the musician score his oratorio, sing it to himself, thrill his own soul, realize what a gift he had to bestow upon his fellows, what a power of inspiration lay in it, and then thrust it into the fire. "Never," you say; "man is not so absolutely demented." But I *have* seen *God* create a world, fill it with innumerable hosts who can think, understand, and delight in Him, inspire them with passionate hungers and thrilling hopes, and then toss it into oblivion, burn them and it into a cinder-heap! You believe it? Then, "I have not found so great faith, no, not in Israel."

II. THIS POWER OF FAITH INHERENT IN HUMAN NATURE IS OUR HOPE. The soil suits the seed that we have to sow. If we fail to convince and win men, it is a proof that we have somehow strangely adulterated our message.

The vast unploughed stretches of Western America had been waiting for centuries for man to till the land and to sow corn in it. There was no need to do more than scratch the surface, and marvellous harvests soon waved over it. The soil was waiting for the seed. And so you may be sure that the human soul is essentially a religious soil. Let us be sure that we have the right seed to sow, and we shall reap harvests that will fill our hearts with gratitude and wonder.

1. The religious faculty is pre-eminently *faith*, and faith is indigenous to the soul of man. That is proved even by the grotesque religions that have been able to secure a hold of him and to fascinate him. When explorers first pushed into the inner regions of Southern Africa, they found everywhere rocks covered with crude attempts at painting. The art was very primitive, but it was genuine art—a proof that even in the rude tribes which dwelt in those uncanny regions the sense of art was alive, and that by-and-by you might perhaps have rivals there of our most brilliant painters. The enthusiast for mathematics descries a mathematician sometimes in the boy who has not passed yet beyond the bounds of the simplest rules of arithmetic. It is enough for him that the mathematical gift is there; he rejoices like a man who has come across a grand opportunity. Given that, and to teach and drill the mind of the boy will be a luxury; he will carry him up in due time to the loftiest heights of his superb science, perhaps live to see his pupil accomplish feats that *he* has never attempted. So let the religious faculty, that is, let the power of faith be in a man—and I hold, let Mr. Le Gallienne say what he pleases, that the faith-faculty is in every man—and there is no height of religious

attainment upon which he may not stand. Agnosticism and Positivism may be poverty-stricken religions, but the Agnostic and the Positivist are both men of "great faith." We pity the idol-worshipper; but faith is strong in him also, a faith which can find some touch of divinity even in the work of his own hands, and you will have in him some day the most striking evidence of the power of Christ.

The story of the gospel gives most convincing illustrations of this in every age. The difficulty is to know which to choose. I have known a man who had spent the bright years of his early manhood in a crusade against the gospel, and yet I felt whenever the man spoke that his soul was steeped in faith, that religion was an absolute necessity to him. And I have seen the same man, after a terrible spiritual convulsion, passionately adore the Lord Jesus and grow to be an ideal disciple. John Bunyan wallowed long in the mires of vulgar sin; but he believed in Jesus, and at his worst quailed before Him, *because* he believed in Him; and the same John Bunyan, mastered, has through the years, by his immortal dream, been fascinating men and leading them from the City of Destruction to the Paradise of God. Augustine in his earlier life was a heathen, but even when a heathen he was a man of faith; religion haunted him long before it became the passion of his life, and when he came under the hand of Jesus, the same faith made him the strong man whose mark is upon the thought of Christendom to this day.

I have seen Joachim stand before a crowded audience, and the hush of a great expectation fell upon every one. There was no sign of timidity in his face; he never seemed to doubt as to whether his music could find them; to him there was a soul of music in every man, and *he* could awake it. So let us never doubt; let there be no hesitation or uncertainty in our message. The faith-faculty is in every man; let us never be afraid that the gospel we have to speak will not find him. The music we have to sing is divine, the voice of God; it will find men, awake and win them. The faith in men will know it when they hear it.

2. To save men is to guide their faith to Him who is the one worthy and fitting Object of it. Having Christ to give them, and having faith, an instinct in every man, you have everything you can ask for; you cannot fail to win them. Paul, wandering about the streets of Athens, found "an altar with this inscription, *To the Unknown God.*" That was enough for Paul. There was a hunger for God, and a craving for a better knowledge of Him, in this people; the spirit of faith was strong in them, and he led them step by step to Jesus.

We possess tremendous advantages to preach Jesus to-day, if we only knew it; man was never so strong in faith, never more eager to find material out of which he can construct a religion in which he can unfeignedly believe. Science has proved to him that there is something in the universe to be absolutely trusted. "Nature," he says, "never lies; she will never deceive me." He sits at her feet like a child at the feet of his mother, listens and chronicles every word she utters. He was never so sensitive to the unseen as to-day; the spiritual world was never such a tangible fact to him. Spiritualism may be crude and confused in its utterances; I confess that I have tried to get hold of some thread which I might be able to draw out of its tangled mass of confident deliverances, and have failed; but it bears witness to man's passion for the unseen, and the immense power of faith in him. Theosophy may be a delusion, but it proves how absolute is man's conviction that the spiritual world is a fact, and how eager is his deepest soul to bring itself in touch with it. The workman who protests that no law of society has the right to call upon him to starve, and who insists that he should have a "living wage," may often act blunderingly and foolishly, but his most frantic cries come from a conviction that, behind this confused puzzle of a world, there is eternal justice, and oh that he could get at it! This is faith. Steeped in faith, soaked in faith, quivering with faith, is man everywhere.

Now, this is the being we have to preach to; and with the Saviour we have to preach, how superb is our chance! Everything he craves for is to be found in Jesus. Jesus is law; Jesus is help; Jesus is right between man and man—right interpreted by love; Jesus is man's craving for immortality made a certainty; Jesus is this sorrow-laden world made the antechamber of heaven; Jesus is God brought within the grasp of man. To preach this Jesus to man with his "great faith" and fail to win him! It is wonderful! We have misunderstood man or misinterpreted the Lord whom we preach, or what is it? Is there something that we have forgotten? Have we stopped too soon?

You remember the scene on Carmel; Elijah, surrounded by the hosts of Israel, standing before the altar with uplifted hands. He had placed the wood thereon, and laid the bullock upon the wood, and his own soul upon that —himself, his work, his devotion to the cause of his God. But he had moved no one yet. The people had heard the prophet's fiery appeal, but they were not convinced as yet. They "answered him not a word." But the prophet lifted up his hands and prayed. And the fire came and consumed the sacrifice, and the people fell upon their faces and cried,

"The Lord, He is the God!" Elijah's message was driven home; they were convinced now. And so you: you have worked and done everything that you could do; you have toiled and taught and pleaded; you have driven the truth home, even convinced those whom you sought to win. But have you prayed? The divine fire alone will convert argument and pleading into a power that will bow every soul before God. Pray, then, pray always, and the Spirit will come and complete the work which you have begun.

THE FATHERHOOD OF GOD.

THE FATHERHOOD OF GOD.

"Our Father."—MATT. vi. 9.

You find the essence of a man's theology in his prayers. Let me hear a man pray, and I will tell you what he believes. It is in your prayers, and not in your arguments, that I look for what your real faith is, for what is food to your soul, for that by which you live.

I have been in a garden of roses, a garden of broad acres where nothing grew but roses—roses of every name and hue; strikingly, brilliantly different, but all roses. And when I left, the owner gave me a small vial of what he called "otto of roses." There were the most striking differences between rose and rose; here and there was a flower of which you could not be quite sure that it was a rose; but this exquisite otto was the quintessence of all the roses, the distilled breath of the garden. And so your creeds and systems of theology may vary. You pass from book to book, from church to church, and you hear arguments, discussions, proofs, that seem to be mutually destructive. But melt them down, distil them, and the truth, the spirit, the quintessence, of them is this—"Our Father." Let the holder of the narrowest theology begin to pray, and he says, "Our Father." Let the broadest theologian, the man who has washed out of his creed what you imagine to be most essential—let him begin to pray, and if he be a Christian at all, he also says, "Our Father." Believe me, you are most yourself not when you argue and speculate, but when you pray, and it is of no use your saying that you have nothing in common with me, if we can kneel together and say, "Our Father." If you gave it to me to write a creed which every Christian might accept, I should search for its items not in the dogmatic pronouncements of the many Churches, but in their prayers.

And now will you look at these old words once again? They have often been your refuge. This is the only prayer to which often you have been able to form your lips; sweeter to you to-day than it has ever been. When you have been baffled and bewildered, when the brain staggered and your heart was faint, you could repeat this, and you had not quite lost God whilst you could. Let us cut these two words once again, and see how much they mean—"Our Father."

I. AND FIRST: THAT IS THE CHRISTIAN DEFINITION OF GOD—"FATHER." Sweet, simple, understandable. Not a definition, perhaps, as the dictionary understands the word "definition." A definition is "a brief description of a thing by its properties," says the dictionary. The Bible seldom attempts definitions in that sense; it certainly never attempts such a definition of God. It invests God with a series of names. He is "Jehovah," "Elohim," "Judge of all the earth;" and the climax, the crown of these names, is "Father;" the last name, the name which expresses, as no other name does, that which is essential in God, as far at least as we are concerned—"Our Father." Look at it.

1. God is a personal Being. I can grasp His hand; I

can look into His face; I can touch Him, love Him, lean hard upon Him. God is not a beautiful idea, a sublime dream, but *Father*.

It has got to be the fashion just now to say that this idea of the personality of God is not at all necessary, that you do not need it. Nobody would think any the less of Shakespeare's Hamlet, we are told, if there had never been an historic Hamlet. The drama would be the same, the waves of emotion it awakes in us, the poet's discussion of the phases of life and love that surge up in it, would be just the same. Nobody stops in reading Homer to say, "These quarrels, spites, and discussions among the deities, these apparitions of gods and goddesses on the field of battle, are an absurdity; there never was a Jupiter or a Saturn, a Venus or a Juno." "What does it matter?" the enthusiast says; "Homer is just as sublime and sweet and majestic, and no one enjoys his poetry any the less for that." Nobody proposes to dismiss the opera because the characters in it are mere myths, mere personified ideas and emotions; nobody enjoys the music any the less for that. And so when you come to religion, "you only want *ideas*," says the man. Mr. Frederic Harrison has just advertised a course of lectures on the "Positivist Creed, Religious, Scientific, Social." Mr. Harrison's conception of what life might be, indeed, of what it is surely going to be, is a noble one. He will talk of virtue, of courage, sobriety, self-denial, worship. Oh yes! worship—for Mr. Harrison worships; and he will talk of God, and if you happened to be there you would wonder, perhaps, what the difference *could* be between his creed and yours. But if you ventured to question, you would find that God to him is only the name he has bestowed upon his grand ideas. The Positivist worships a blank, worships his *dream*. God is merely a sublime name around which he has gathered a number of inspiring ideas.

Now listen : "*Our Father ;*" not ideas, dreams, sublime conceptions of duty, but some one in whom the dream lives, breathes, is embodied. Oh, I can appreciate the Positivist's wonderfully eloquent talk about virtue and self-denial and purity, and the duty of moral self-culture. It is infinitely higher than the base, vulgar materialism which practically says that there is no such thing as virtue, and that the man who denies himself for another's sake is a fool. I can understand the fascination of Pantheism. I can appreciate Mr. Swinburne's brilliant and half-bewitching poetry; his exquisite poem in one of this month's magazines is a song of the purest and loftiest genius. The picture of the pine forest which to him has become a temple—

"A temple whose transepts are measured by miles,
  Whose chancel has morning for priest "—

is one of the loveliest and most perfect touches in modern poetry. But pure Pantheism fails even him. He has had to find some personal divinity for the shrine of his devotions, and so dedicates his hymn to his mother. And so I. The poet's hymn thrills me; I shall henceforth hear voices in the pine-forest which I have never heard before; but it is a mockery to call it a temple if there be nothing but ministrants. The temple must have its divinity as well as its ministrants; an ear to hear, an eye to see, a heart to feel, a hand to help, must have its God. I am sad and sorrowful and sinful, and sometimes well-nigh broken-hearted, and my God must be—well, what?

I will tell you. I was standing not long ago by a child's sick-cot; and if there is any sight which it is hard to look upon, it is that of the little one, to whom it is all such a mystery, racked and tortured with pain. But the brave little heroine whispered, "Father, give me your hand;" and holding her father's hand, though riddled with pain, she never moaned. And so I. I do not know what others may not be able to do; I criticize no one, think hard thoughts of no one; I only say that in my bewilderments, sorrows, heartaches, struggles, I cannot rest upon ideas, visions, aspirations, strivings. I say, " Father, give me Thine hand." I can be patient and brave then. Father! "Our Father!"

2. God is touched, moved, is not indifferent to me and my condition—me and the battles that I have to fight. "Our Father." You dare not always be sure as to what God's feelings towards you may be, as to how much you may mean to God. Sometimes you try to guess. You ask Nature. She shakes her head, and you cannot be sure as to what she means; whether it is that she does not know, or that she does know but will keep the secret to herself. Sometimes the look of Him which you find in Nature frightens, appalls you. It is not always you can delight in Nature. Her very grandeur and sublimity sometimes seem cruel to you. "Gracious Nature," says Professor Ray Lankester—" man yearns towards her, knowing her to be his dear mother." I am not so sure of that; she sometimes seems to be little better than a harsh and ruthless stepmother. Wordsworth loved her, and has taught more men to love her than all the poets put together; but even Wordsworth tells us in one of his noblest poems of the scene on the lake when her very majesty terrified him, and he shrank into himself. You read the Bible, and you are not always quite sure as to what place you have in His thoughts. You stand away as Israel did, awed and

abashed; were He to speak to you, your soul would quake. Like Elijah, you bow your head; hushed if not subdued. You can never lift up your eyes and be sure of what you must be to Him until you come here. "Our Father"— that settles everything, that makes it an absolute certainty; you know now where you stand with regard to Him; not callous nor indifferent to you is He.

Wait there for a moment. Very little place will the world give you in its thoughts, if it can help it; and if it is compelled to think of you, its thoughts will not be always benedictions. Sometimes it will be jealous of you. You little guess, you younger souls, its capacity for jealousy; you little dream how it can criticize you; how stinging is its tongue, how bitter it can be. Do you intend to write a book? Every author of every small pamphlet will remind you how poor are its arguments, how bald is its style. Would you be a painter? I would not be a *great* painter, if I were you. Every miserable daubster will know how poor your drawing is, how commonplace your ideas; or, if not commonplace, he will know where you stole them from. Or, will you go up to business? I would not work too hard or push to the front, if I were you. Every man who has been too indolent to work, or too dull to have made much of it even if he had not been indolent, will shrug his shoulders, and hint that you have succeeded because you have been hard and unscrupulous, and even worse, if the truth were told. Jealous! Oh, the world has a wonderful gift of jealousy. And when it is not jealous, how indifferent, how pitiless, it can be! What will the world care for you when it can get no more out of you? Serve it, sell yourself to suit its purposes, and it will make much of you; but when you have broken down under your burden, the world will leave you to die in the hedge; will squeeze you as dry as a sponge, suck you as dry as an orange, and then toss you away with contempt.

But—*father!* Dear young people whom I love, young students who are just beginning your career, brave young fellows who are just setting your hand to business, there is one at least pledged to you, to whom your success will mean more than it can mean to you, to whom it will be worth more than his own success could be—your father. Henry the English king stood watching his son in the stress of the battle. Messengers came urging the king to send help to the young warrior. "Nay," said the king, "let him win his spurs." But the king watched the battle the whole day through, saw nothing that day but his son's plume in the thick of the fight. And you, young men and women—your fathers and mothers see nothing but you. They give you large liberty; they trust you. You are winning your spurs. But they watch, and are often anxious; they pray and hold their breath. I would not disappoint them, if I were you; I would not be a rake, or an idler, or a spendthrift, if I were you. I would be a *man.* I would not be frivolous, shallow-souled, and empty-headed, if I were you. I would be a godly *woman.* Listen: "Our Father." I am in the battle; I often feel as if I were hedged in by powers bent upon my destruction. Forms of thought that bewilder me; books the authors of which seem to have said, "The man who reads this shall believe nothing, I will cut him adrift from every shore;" business temptations that make it hard for you to maintain your integrity. Ah! God sees the stress of the battle; the eye of God is upon us; God will never allow us to be overwhelmed. "Our Father."

3. The God to whom it is our right to come and tell our tale. Every one is glad to receive you when you are prosperous. Make money, and the world will do its best to persuade you that you are wise and virtuous. Publish a successful book, and every one will want you to be his guest. Show that there is a flash of the mysterious fire which the world calls genius in you, and men will compete to shake hands with you. Be a Zola, and you shall be regaled with flattery. Literary clubs will talk of you as the " Imperator Maximus in the beautiful kingdom of ideas." Bah!—beautiful kingdom of the slums and sewers! His last-week flatterers may imagine that he has "made conquest of France, of Europe, of England, and even Mrs. Grundy." Why, England—real England—loathes, spues from it every book tainted with the slime that seems to be so sweet to this brilliant man; England has not yet begun to believe that filth is genius. But one must acknowledge that you have only to succeed and become famous, and the world will only too seldom ask what the inspiration of your life is. But it shrinks from those who fail, pretends to have forgotten them. And the majority of us *have* failed. Oh yes, we have! We have not realized our dreams; we did not mean once to walk behind the crowd, the last almost of those who started with us. Our religion, even for some of us, has become poor, meagre, thin. Our beautiful enthusiasms have died down. Hearts which once blazed with hope have lost the courage to expect. We live still in the memory of what life once promised to be, but we have become slow-footed, and the burden is heavy.

I was at a house once when the boy who had left home to do wonders returned. He had entered college with *éclat*, fame had already begun to repeat his name, and I was at the door when he came back and said—and oh, the weariness in his face!—" Father, I have come home to die." *You* have not come to that yet; you have not been even beaten yet. But you are sad and weary and disappointed. Oh, if you could only pour out your soul for once—tell how life looks to you; if you could only get a good cry! Come here, tell it here. Life is getting to choke you. Tell it now; take up the old prayer; begin with " Our Father."

II. AGAIN: WE HAVE HERE AN EXPOSITION—THE REASON OF THE STORY OF OUR REDEMPTION. All that I have said so far covers very little of what "fatherhood" implies. That God should be concerned for us and pity us, that we should have the right of access to Him, we take as matters of course. But "fatherhood" implies much more than that. It implies every line of the gospel story, from the first dawn of hope in Eden to "the consummation of all things" in the second Eden. The wealth and wonder of the story sometimes makes it unbelievable, but that there should be no story of redemption would be still more unbelievable. If you begin with "Our Father," redemption follows as a matter of course. To begin with—

1. To save man was to God a *necessity*. To *serve* our children is even a necessity to us. We toil for them; we coin our strength into sacrifice to make the pathway into life easier for them. Hard work is bread to us when we are working for the children. They shall enjoy the richest helps of education; they shall know what culture means— it shall broaden, deepen, and sweeten their life. But fatherhood covers much more than that; you have not done everything when you have done that. Your son returns from the university enriched with every gift, invested in every grace with which the university can endow him,

fitted for work, and none of life's opportunities will be lost upon him. You have served him well, and it is your proud boast that everything a father could do for his son you have done for yours. But you have never spoken to him on the highest subject of all; diffident, you have hesitated, stuttered, and stammered; but you have never spoken. On the great subject, the subject of subjects, you have been silent. You have done nobly, but you have not touched perfect fatherhood.

But turn to God. God has gloriously served me, but God could never tell His concern for me by anything less than *saving* me; the wealth of His love, His real concern for me, would be still untold. That is perfect fatherhood.

Let me give you an illustration. Robert Browning has an exquisite little poem which he calls "One Word More." The idea of the poem is this. One of the greatest, perhaps *the* greatest Italian artist, who is already a painter, feels that there is more in him than painting can express, and from sheer necessity he takes to sculpture. Not that he gives up painting; but he adds sculpture to it, in order to relieve his own soul, that he might put into marble what he could not put on the canvas. Browning compares himself to that artist in addressing the wife whom he loved with such adoring self-abandonment. He had addressed her in verse, but what verse could express the love that was his? And he longs for some other art than poetry to tell the one word more that was in him. And so here. God had *served* man, created a perfect home for man—served his intellect, quickened it by the problems which He had set him to solve; but He still needed the "one word more" to tell all that was in Him. None of these things could tell His love—tell the depth of it; the *necessity* that man was to Him.

2. That necessity has found voice for itself in the Cross, in the Atonement. Pray do not expect me to expound or discuss that Atonement. Be content just now with what lies in the direct line of my subject. The Atonement is the full expression of the Divine Fatherhood; God found full voice for Himself in it.

The poet has tried many subjects, has given hints of the wealth of soul there is in him, but has never found full voice for himself yet. Tennyson had sung many minor poems before the " In Memoriam " came. We knew that he was a rare singer, a master-poet; but we never knew till then that he was much more than a singer—that he was a teacher, a prophet, a man who could break the spell of our doubts. Handel was born a musician—he told himself in much memorable music; but he never found full utterance for himself until he poured the whole store of his genius into the " Messiah." There is the ecstasy of a soul that has found a subject big enough for itself in the rich, triumphant choruses of that. The patriot had always loved his country; those who knew him knew that its name was engraven on his heart. But no one knew—he himself had never known—the depth of his love nor the wealth of his resources until dire disaster had fallen upon the land. He suddenly discovered himself, and half hailed his country's woe, for it gave him the chance to tell himself. And God—*His love for man*—He had always told it to the few that understood; told it in the beauty of the world in which He had set man to live, in the patience that had borne with man in face of all his wickedness—a patience that refused to be beaten, that refused to be discouraged. But the wealth of His love, the hunger of His heart for man, the necessity man was to Him, was never told but on the cross. And the Cross is only "Our *Father*" fully translated.

3. From this necessity which it is to Him to save us He will not allow us to escape. In his Fatherhood He will follow us with ministries of love, pursue us with sore chastisement, baptize us with "fire and brimstone" if need be. Oh, He is not easily discouraged; you will find it hard to weary Him. I have just read a remarkable poem, which the author calls "The Hound of Heaven." The "Hound of Heaven" is the love of Christ. It pursues men everywhere, torments them, hunts them down. Do what they will, they cannot escape it. They hide themselves in thickets of infidelity; read every book which takes to prove that Jesus is a myth, or that in any case the claims He makes for Himself are preposterous. But the "Hound of Heaven," the love of Christ, hunts them down. They plunge themselves into the waters of forgetfulness, wallow in the mires of sensuality, do mad things, if by any means they may forget and get rid of Jesus. But the "Hound of Heaven" finds them even there. I wonder whether any of you are trying to do that? I have looked in wonder at the life you have chosen, the pleasures which you profess at least to satisfy yourselves with. Oh, you have never succeeded—even *I* can see that! I have seen you here on a Sunday morning; you had absolutely forgotten yourselves; you knew nothing of what the preacher was saying, and there was a scare which was half despair in your faces. Oh, if you could only get rid of the love of Christ, this "Hound of Heaven"! But no; once again it had run you down. And even if you harden yourself, and take

upon you to prove that you are free by casting your lot with those upon whom the doom of hell has fallen, do you know what hell means? It is a man failing to forget that God is his Father; running away for ever from God—running away from the thought, dogged for ever by the remembrance that God is his Father, and must love him, hunger for him even yet. Oh, if he could only lay the awful burden down; if he could only seal his ears and escape from the torment of it; if he could only drink of the waters of Lethe and forget! "Our Father!"—he said it often in his childhood on his knees; it was his heaven then, it has become his hell now.

What am I saying? The Fatherhood of God a terrible thought? Misused, it is the most terrible of all thoughts. But it shall never become a terror to you, shall it? Set yourself right with God this morning, so that it shall become an ever more blessed thought to you that God can never cease to be your Father. "Our Father."

III. LASTLY: THIS IS THE GROUNDWORK OF OUR GRANDEST HOPES FOR THE HEREAFTER. Immortality becomes a certainty to us as we repeat these two words. There are many ways of proving that we are to continue to be. I know all the great arguments from Cicero's down to that of the modern Christian evolutionist. But I will tell you how I argue; I find my argument in this—

1. Our immortality is a necessity to God, a necessity to "Our Father." A necessity to me? you ask. Well, yes, as a rule. But I will confess to you, not always. Oh, I have been afraid of it; it has been a terror and not a joy to me. I have prayed for blank nothingness—for the sleep that should know no awaking; I have longed to cease to be. But I have recovered myself, and remembered that it was a

necessity to *Him;* and that it is a necessity to Him is the one argument that never breaks down.

Shall I tell you the moods in which immortality becomes a necessity to me? I have used all the big arguments in my time, like other people; talked of my soul's insatiable craving for knowledge; the vision of moral perfection which I have had in inspired moments has become a blessedness which is half torture, and I have longed to stand some day before God "without spot, or wrinkle, or any such thing"—a fit comrade for His noblest sons. But there have been hours when knowledge was a mockery; when you might have burnt all books and I would not have lifted my hand to prevent you; when spiritual failure had become painful disaster, a shame and a humiliation, and I had no heart to persevere. Immortality was no necessity to me then; I even shrank from it. But even then humbler necessities keep a fire of hope flickering in me. The spell of my early days is often upon me; I become young again, and I crave for "the touch of the vanished hand, and the sound of the voice that is still." Oh, angels of my childhood, I *must* have you again! I have children who have woven themselves about my heart-strings and created in me new hungers, who have lighted a fire in me which I protest should never be put out. Christmas will not be here for two months and more, but you are beginning to count the hours already, for the boys are coming home. And even God—shall I dare say it? yes, I will—*God* must have His children about Him; eternity would become a burden even to Him without us. With my last breath I will pray no prayer but this—the prayer I prayed at my mother's knee—"Our Father," for that will be a pledge to me that I shall awake yonder.

2. That immortality will be one of pure blessedness. I

sometimes try to forecast the future, to draw aside the veil, to anticipate the unseen, and to imagine what it will be to be "for ever with the Lord." But I am perfectly content to wait; it is enough for me that the home shall be what my Father has provided. You remember the old school and college days, or the days when necessity banished you to the other side of the globe to gain a footing for yourself in life; you remember, after months, perhaps years, of absence, coming home again; you remember seeking the old room, and finding every wish and taste of yours anticipated. Every book said, "Some one who knows and loves me has been here." The flowers on the table, fresh from the old garden, greeted you, and in every corner was some sweet surprise. You sat down to think and to drink it all in, and you said, "My mother has done this, God bless her! there is no place like home." And so you dream of the home eternal sometimes. You construct the future; imagination builds "the temple not made with hands;" heaven unlocks all its stores, unfolds all its wonders, for you; and you become young again as you dream. But these dreams are only breaks; you only rest yourself in the dream for a moment. You set yourself to work again, to serve your day, to leave the world in something richer than you found it. Heaven is the "Father's house." That is enough: let Him prepare your place for you.

OUR SALVATION INTELLIGIBLE IN THE LIGHT OF GOD'S LOVE.

OUR SALVATION INTELLIGIBLE IN THE LIGHT OF GOD'S LOVE.

"God is love."—1 JOHN iv. 8.

GLORIOUS words; but the most terrible text in the Bible to preach from. I will confess to you—I am half afraid of it. I have seen a brilliant musician, a brilliant executant at the piano; I have seen him drop his hands when he came to the supreme passage in the grand composition which he was interpreting. It would be desecration, a crime, he feels, to spoil it; and his courage fails him. I feel exactly so here. I have been preaching now for many years, but I have never ventured to take these words as a text before. Even now I am half afraid of them. You are perfectly welcome to criticize me as a rule; but lay a charge upon yourselves this morning that you will not criticize. Let us go together and *look* at this. "God is love." And now, the first thing that strikes us is that—

I. IN THE SIGHT OF GOD MAN IS A BEING OF UNSPEAKABLE WORTH. And the fact is only intelligible—the language in which God speaks of man is only intelligible—in the light of this first fact, "God is *love*." It is very easy to prove the insignificance, the contemptibleness, of man.

The scientist, for instance, traces him to the ape, and says, "This is where he came from;" or he dissects his brain, and says, "Thought, emotion, love, imagination, poetry, worship,—see the marks of every one of them upon this material tablet, which we call the brain." The dramas of Shakespeare, the hymns in which we have this morning spoken our gratitude, our awe, our delight in God, are nothing but the quiverings of this sensitive grey substance —the brain. And this gospel story—the cynic indulges in cheap sneers at it, and asks if you are going to make an angel out of this sorry being with his vulgar appetites and animal lusts. It is very easy to sneer, though you should remember that you prove nothing by shrugging your shoulders. The sober-minded Deist, out of pure reverence for God, he thinks, refuses to believe the story. That the infinite God should concern Himself with man and his paltry destiny is incredible. The brain in which such an idea was born had lost the sense of the proportion of things. And it *is* incredible. Man *is* so small, mean, ignoble, unworthy, until you read his story with the eyes of love; until you remember this—"*God* is *love.*" But listen. Every mother is bewitched and colour-blind. She will waste the wealth of her brave heart upon the boy in whom no one but herself can see one sign of grace or virtue. But it is a luxury to *her* to serve him. The Christian philanthropist who works in the mire of Whitechapel, where, as my friend who is here this morning frankly said the other day at Lambeth, it is impossible for hosts who are crowded into its ugly conditions to live sweet, pure lives, where a man *cannot* be a Christian, seeks for pearls even there. The man who believes in no prophet but the political economist thinks that Christian philanthropy is sheer infatuation, sheer waste of human energy. And so it *is* to everything but *love*. But let Browning speak to you—

> "Love greatens and glorifies all things,
> Till God is aglow to the loving heart,
> In what was mere earth before."

Love sees worth in what to every other eye is contemptible. And so when you come to think of man. I never quarrel with any one who contends for pure materialism, and who laughs because we set such worth upon what is nothing more than organized protoplasm to him. I simply say, "Quite so, my dear sir." I never dream of answering when the political economist talks of the wastefulness of Christian enthusiasm, or the infatuation of men who spend themselves in the many devices of Christian philanthropy. Drunken, sin-sodden, irredeemable man, sacrifice is wasted upon him. Exactly; but—

> "God is aglow to the loving heart,
> In what was mere earth before."

The poorest, wretchedest, most sin-sodden is to God a mirror in which He sees Himself. Beautiful, of infinite worth to Him! Divine to Him, for "God is *love*."

II. GOD SEEKS FOR EVERY MAN THE MOST PERFECT DESTINY; THE MOST PERFECT GOOD. And the most perfect good of man, as interpreted by God, is no small, mean, niggardly thing. Shall I say two things concerning that?

1. The good of man includes the whole man. It includes the body. To preach the gospel of health is to preach the gospel of Jesus Christ. God intended us to die as the ripe fruit falls from the tree. The physician is God's servant, as well as the preacher. Every true physician has a gospel to preach, as well as the man who takes his texts

from the Bible. Nature is a Bible as well as this Book, and Dr. Richardson is as truly God's servant as any man who stands up in a pulpit to-day. It includes the mind. God claims every pure-minded writer as His workman. The painter who gets intoxicated with the wine of nature, and the musician whose music is not an echo, but a translation of his own soul,—each of them is God's ordained priest. Every one of them—poet, painter, musician; ay, even the mathematician,—wears his ephod. It includes the sunniest as well as the gloomiest sides of human life. The frosts of winter work for the harvest. So still more do the showers of spring and the summer sunshine. It is well to be grave, but it is also well to be merry. The serious face of the earnest-minded man is comely; but so also is the sunshine in the face of the boy, and the laughter of a little child is sweet as a hymn in the ear of God.

2. But these things are preliminaries. They exist merely for the sake of a greater thing than themselves. Beyond these there is something still sacreder and more precious. These are but pathways that lead to a still holier shrine—the spirit; that which knows God, feeds upon God, looks into the face of God, worships God. Here man finds his most perfect good, and God works *through* every other good to this.

Wait there for a moment. There lies the difference between divine love and human love. *We* ignore the highest for the sake of the lowest. We ruin our children in the name of the vulgarest and ignoblest thing in them, and we imagine that to be love. The child's native indolence grumbles against the drill and what he calls the hard work of the school. "Poor overtaxed boy!" says the mother, "I must not permit it;" and he grows up with a flabby mind that is not fit for such a world as this. "Children *must* move in society," say the overfond father and doting mother; "our Puritan fathers were wrong, the old Puritan idea was fanaticism." And the children form habits for which they have no real liking; but society must be obeyed. Reading ceases, and religious exercises which were once a delight become a weariness.

There are not half a dozen of you here this morning who would not toss any religious service on one side in the name of a dance or the last frivolous fiat of society, whatever that may be.

I often saw in Upper Egypt an ancient temple pulled to pieces to build a village of hovels. I have seen a band of roving gipsies tear down the exquisitely carved panels of an old palace to light a fire to boil their kettle with. And I have seen young people—*my* young people, who belong to me by every right—I have seen them take their books, take the studies in which they had been long immersed, and with them light the fires of sordid pleasures and the many foolishnesses of fashionable life. I have seen those who were once enthusiastic Sunday-school teachers tear up their work and pile it on the fire. I have seen old friends of mine here give up the house of God; I have seen them take the Table of the Lord at which they had often sat and seen the Lord, take up their whole religious life, with its glorious memories, and pile it on the fire—on the fire of a world that was living "without God and without hope." *We* use the highest to light the lowest. Not so God. God also has His fire; and the fire is your religious life. And God uses your whole soul, your whole nature, to supply fuel for that fire. Your intellectual life; you read, you think; but you read and think that you may have fuel for the fire. You go through the drill of your daily work, you wrestle with temptations; it is fuel for the fire. You join hands with others in the joy of worship. The Word of God feeds you, the common hymn and the common prayer thrill you; it is all fuel for the fire. This is man's highest good as God reads it; this God feeds, for "*God* is *love.*"

III. GOD HAS MADE SUFFICIENT PROVISION TO SECURE EVERY MAN'S HIGHEST GOOD. There is a very famous English poem—of course you know who wrote it—it is called "Pictor Ignotus," the painter who chose to remain unknown; the man of genius, the born painter, who refused to paint because men would not understand, would not properly appreciate his work. He shrank, as every sensitive man would shrink, from having his work bought by vulgar men, to be hung up in their galleries or on their dining-room walls, not because they cared for art, but because it was the fashionable thing to patronize art, and prove your wealth by the pictures with which you lined your walls. He shuddered at the thought. He would never degrade the genius that was in him by pandering to vulgar wealth. He would go on holding fellowship with his own soul's visions in the soul's private sanctuary; but he would not demean himself by selling his soul to the man who merely could pay the highest price for it. But that is not the noblest genius. Real genius *must* express itself, even for its own sake. Forgive the illustration. God *must* express Himself for His own sake. God has poured out the wealth of His redemption. We may reject it or receive it: God *must* give it. God must sing the song of His own heart. He wrote it in the lives of heroes; spoke it from the lips of prophets; told the wealth of it in the life and death of Jesus. He has been telling it unweariedly through the ages. Men

IN THE LIGHT OF GOD'S LOVE.   163

have rejected it, scorned it, treated it with contempt. It matters not: to God to tell Himself was a necessity, for "God is *love*."

1. Now, first there. In the redemption of man God has found a work by which He may fully express Himself. The famous Oriental scholar, whom all Europe knows, wrote more than one book before we understood what a unique and wealthy-minded man he was. "Chips from a German Workshop" he called them. Every one of them showed the sign-manual of the rare scholar who knew the way to think. But these were only his recreations. By-and-by he published the grand idea, to work out which had been the business of his life. It was through this that he revealed the real man he was. So men talk of the wonders of *nature*. They often become so absorbed in nature that they have no wish to look beyond it. But these were the mere trifles of God's works. God had never been able to tell Himself in these. Job saw them and exclaimed—the words might be taken as the motto to be written on the title-page of every science text-book—"Lo! these are but the outskirts of His ways; and how small a whisper do we hear of Him?" Stand out under the stars to-night: if you are poets, you *may* sing; if you are not poets, you can worship. Count them—flecks of foam floating on the infinite tide past the feet of God. Look, until your soul becomes deeper than the heavens above you, and as hushed as the heavens. Read the world's many Bibles. Read Mahomet, read Gautama, read Moses. For myself, I delight in every one of them. But every inspired man the world has ever known, every gospel which has ever cheered man—and oh! Gautama, Mahomet, Moses, the message of each of them has been a gospel to somebody—were only

sparks from the anvil at which God was working, chips from the infinite workshop, God's minor ideas. But Christ came; Calvary came. *This* is God; this was the solution of the world's problem: God had told Himself at last. Pardon, hope, life, for all the world; the break of the eternal day. *This* is God.

And now—

2. The love of God makes it all credible. It would be impossible to believe it did we not know that "God is *love.*" Do you know that the pith of a thing, the glory of a thing, is often the incredible thing about it, often the thing that is hardest to believe? Every one believes the Bible to be a marvellous book. Even those who will not make it the law of their life compete with one another as to who shall say the most complimentary word in its praise. It is a unique *literature;* and the world is getting to study it as a wonderful literature, to read it for the charm of it, as the world has read the Greek and Roman classics. It is when you begin to talk of the book as inspired, begin to contend that God is in it as He is in no other book, that He moved men to write it for a specific purpose, that men hesitate. Every one *believes* in Jesus. Oh yes, everybody does. Matthew Arnold did; Renan did; Dr. Martineau does. Every one, in a sense, *adores* Him. It is when you speak of the Cross, when you speak of the "Lamb of God," of the sins of the world being laid upon Him, that men begin to hesitate and stammer. "No, no; that is incredible; that can never be," they say. But love—the love of God—makes even that—makes every item of the story credible. I have seen the miracles that love works. I have seen a poor woman clemming that the children might have enough

to eat. I have seen a man bid his son good-bye, knowing that he should never see his face again, and sending him out to the mission-field. And I see God bearing the sins of the world; Jesus bowing His head under the awful tragedy. I protest—I hate it—it is an ugly sight. Hush! the Cross shall be for ever the symbol of love's perfect triumph. It was *love*, it was LOVE that did it. "God is *love*."

I had one other point; but I must limit myself to a sentence on that point.

IV. GOD WILL WORK OUT THE PROVISIONS THAT HE HAS MADE SO THAT THEY SHALL NOT MISS WHAT THEY AIM AT. Set it down as a certainty that God's love will win, that the gospel of love will tell. But I must not trust myself to go after that. One word must suffice.

This love often uses terrible means to secure its purpose. Do not miss that. Not terrible means for the sake of using them, but terrible means because it will not submit to be beaten. Terrible disasters require terrible remedies; but he who can use terrible remedies, loves. I was at Doulton's wonderful art works the other afternoon. I have believed in London more since then than I had ever done before, though I have always believed in London. I am almost the only one among you who ventures to say that there are glorious art treasures in London; that we have buildings which prove that the Englishman has the true architectural instinct. I believe in London, though I have seen Venice. But there was one superb specimen of art there—an illustration of a dream of Dante's. I was admiring the figure of Beatrice—the exquisite workmanship, the pose and grace of the figure. "Ah," said the gentleman who was showing it to me, "that has to be *fired* three times yet; those colours must be made permanent." So is it with some of you. You have been sore tried; but God set so much store upon the design He is cutting into you, that He may set you in the fire even yet. He will not miss His aim; for "God is love."

READING.

READING.

"Till I come, give attendance to reading."—1 TIM. iv. 13.

THIS is Paul's advice to Timothy—the advice of an old man to a young man; of an old *minister*, as we should say to-day, to a young minister.

Paul had himself been a great reader. A reader of the Hebrew Scriptures—that goes without saying; a reader of Jewish theology—no one but a theologian, no one but a *Jewish* theologian, no one upon whom Jewish theology had not left its mark, could have written the Epistle to the Galatians. Some of the Jewish theologian's tricks of speech, the expressions which only a Jewish theologian would have used, his fondness for the allegory, all come out in Paul.

Paul had been a great reader of Greek philosophy. It was only a man who had once been steeped in Greek metaphysics that could have written the Epistle to the Colossians, and it requires a metaphysician still to expound it and to preach it. Paul was a reader of the poets. The Greek poets we know, I have no doubt he knew; but he knew minor poets we have never read. He quoted the poets in his sermons. He knew how to arrest an audience, and in preaching to the Greeks at Athens he quoted their own poets to them.

In all his wanderings, in all his missionary journeyings, he never forgot his books. Imprisoned in Rome, he longed for his books. Writing from prison, in another letter to Timothy, who was proposing to go to see him, he says, "The cloak that I left at Troas with Carpus, bring when thou comest, *and the books.*" If Paul were delivering a charge to a young minister to-day, one thing you may depend upon it he would say—"Read." And what he would say to the young minister, he would say to every youth and maiden here—"Give attendance to reading."

I have three things to say — or rather, I will try to answer three questions: Why? What? How?

I. And first, WHY READ? Wherein lies the importance of reading? Why should it be so necessary for you to read?

1. Books are the treasure-houses of ideas; the record of man's many attempts to solve the problem of his own existence, of the thoughts that have come to him as he pondered over himself, and over the majestic and awful and, in any case, beautiful universe in the midst of which he finds himself placed. Physiologists tell me that every idea that flits through my mind leaves the record of itself in my brain—leaves a line on the material tablet; just as the music you sing into the phonograph leaves a dent there, and, if you only know how to manage it, you can reproduce the music at your leisure. I do not know as to that; but books *are* a record. I read only yesterday one of the sermons I preached here twenty years ago—I was young and foolish then, and never hesitated to publish—and I asked in wonder, "Did I ever say this; could I ever have thought this?" And I want sometimes to know what men thought and dreamt, what the universe meant to them five hundred

or a thousand years ago. What did life signify to the wisest and best then? What hopes had they? What was their inspiration as they fronted duty? What did they feel when death robbed them of their strongest and their best? What did men say in the early morning of the world, when the Silent Figure whom there was no resisting touched them, and they had to pass under the veil into the unseen? I open my books and I have the record. I know what the bravest and the best have thought, dreamt, and tried to be. Oh, great books into which men have distilled the quintessence of their ideas, guesses, desires, aspirations, the quintessence of what they *were*, the very flavour of their souls,—I am never poor or lonely whilst I have you. I live in every age, am the contemporary of every era; I talk with all the prophets, and every one who has helped the world, refreshes me.

Books do this in a sense in which nothing else does. The art-gallery, to be sure, is a history. The collection of paintings by the old masters which is on exhibition in London just now will help you to realize what England was in the years covered by that exhibition. If you know how to read those pictures, you will see what that generation's ideal of beauty was; you will see the point which civilization had reached. I spend an hour sometimes with the Greek sculptures in the British Museum. When I come away, Greece has soaked me, saturated me, taken possession of me; I half unconsciously think Greek; I understand how ardently the Greek worshipped physical strength, litheness, and beauty. But none of these things are what a book is. It is into their books that the great representative souls of the race have put their dreams, their passions, their endeavours, their aspirations. The thinking, the prayers, the devotions of the world, argued in books, sung in books, enshrined in books—the great, rich, royal, indestructible treasure-houses of the world!

2. Books stimulate you to think. Thinking, mind you, is a very different matter from the mere acquiring of facts. The most learned people are often the ineptest thinkers. It does not follow for a moment that because you are a scholar, because you can run off a countless number of facts, that you can *think*. The dullest people the world has ever known have often been the most brilliant *scholars*, and no one can be so absolutely dull as the scholar who is dull. But if you know the way to use it, there is nothing that can stir you to think like a living book. Indeed, that is the test by which I try a book; if it does not stir you to think, I decline to call it a book. The value of a book, the power of a book, is not what it gives you, but what it enables you to get for yourself; that it awakes you, stirs you up; that when you have read it you are alive to your soul's deepest depths. Every faculty you possess is roused, your soul quivers, and whatever there is in you discovers itself.

The match does not create the fire, but lights it. You have gathered the materials of a fire; there is wood there and coals—the material out of which a fire is made—but it may lie there for a century and never become a fire. But strike a match, and your fire will soon be burning. The magnetic battery *gives* you nothing, but it stirs up the latent forces that lie in you and which have gone to sleep. The breezy walk across the hills or the drive along the sea-beach added nothing to the bulk of your body. Oxygen and ozone are not food, but they enabled you to use and digest your food. They sweetened and purified your blood.

Health, vigour, energy were yours again, and health, vigour, energy mean life. So the book—so all the *best* books; their worth is not what they give you, but what they enable you to become. Byron always used to read before he began to write. An idea had struck him, and he roused his mind, stirred himself up to do justice to the idea, gave himself the start by reading some great book, the composition of one of the master-minds. This moved him, fully awakened him; his whole soul was alive, and he poured out the best that was in him then. One of the most remarkable preachers London ever knew, once said that he never heard George Dawson speak, but he went home determined to produce something greater than he had ever done before —to preach a better sermon, to touch a point in preaching that he had never reached; and he almost always did. Now, that is the sign of the great book—and if I were you I would never, except on very rare occasions, when the mind, like the body, needed recreation, read anything but a great book—it will stir you up and give you to yourself at your best; you will be able to *think* when you have read the true book. The true book is the match that lights the fire; it is the battery that stimulates the mind to activity; it is the mountain breeze—the oxygen, the ozone—that sets the mind in health, so that everything it does is at its best.

3. Books will show you the real worth of what you yourself have thought. Every young man is self-confident, opinionated, conceited; indeed, he would not be worth much if he were not. I understood things better than everybody else when I was one and twenty. I was perfectly ready, at half an hour's notice, to set any Church assembly right on any matter. I sit down quietly now and laugh at the over-

weening bombast of my sermons of twenty years ago. I have kept a few of them, which I read in my diffident moods, and reproach myself with having lost my daring and self-confidence, and ask, "Why cannot you be dogmatic to-day as you used to be?" Oh, it was right to be infallible at one and twenty; the mistake is to remain at one and twenty to the end of your days—to be one and twenty at fifty, sixty, seventy. But truth is great and many-sided. You stand under the hush of heaven with its teeming worlds at midnight, you shrink under the grandeur of it, its sublimity over-awes you, and you become ashamed as you watch that you have ever been bombastic. And so the awful majesty of the great questions—God and the destiny of this soul of mine, and how I am to realize the chief good—sinks into me, and I bow my head. Prate, talk confidently here! Talk as if the truth in all its completeness existed in this little brain of mine! The ignorance, the audacity, the impertinence of it! Let me know what others have thought and guessed, the form in which others have held it. Let me read, or I shall inevitably become a bigot, become small and narrow-minded—the one thing I should be ashamed to become.

For instance, here is this Bible. What, exactly, is it? What am I to mean when I say it is inspired? What is to be the destiny of man; what lies before him beyond the veil which we call death? The Cross—ah! that is what I want to understand; the Atonement. Oh! I hold my own; I have the clearest conception in my own mind as to what it means; all my hopes are centred in it, all my doubts drop, and the love of God becomes a glorious certainty as I look at it; but I never imagine that I know the whole truth concerning it that I can give a full exposition of it.

"In the cross of Christ I glory," "God forbid that I should glory, *save* in the cross of our Lord Jesus Christ;" but when I have said my last word about it, I always feel inclined to sit down and say, "Now will some of you stand up and say what *you* see in it?" And I go to every book, and I always find that it has some fresh thing to say about the cross, has seen something in it that I had never seen.

I have roamed through the region of which Mont Blanc is the centre. I could see the mountain twenty miles away as I approached it by the Tête Noir Pass; every line of it cut against a cloudless sunset. I have looked at it through the ever-changing mists, which for ever broke and closed in again as if to taunt one, at Chamounix. I have looked back at it as I drove towards Geneva, and it seemed to say, "You have not seen my last glory yet." Wonderful, majestic still, but not what it had been, viewed from other standpoints. It is only the man who has seen the monarch mountain from every side and in all its moods that can say that he knows it. And so, I seek to look at the cross from every standpoint. I have read every book that I could get at that had anything to say about it. John Calvin has described it. Even the cross looked half grim from where he stood, but it *was* the cross. And McLeod Campbell and Mr. Spurgeon have described it, and each has shown me something new and precious beyond price in it. I read and for ever read. I hail every fresh standpoint from which I can see it. I shall be able to cheer myself by-and-by with the thought that I *know* it.

Why read? Well, there are at least those three reasons. First, books are the treasure-houses of ideas; secondly, books stimulate you to think; thirdly, books show you the comparative worth of what you have thought. That first.

II. And then, secondly, WHAT SHALL I READ?

1. Read what will cover your whole nature, cover every side of your soul. Dr. Storrs—perhaps the finest preacher living—in advising brother-preachers as to what to read, summing up his brilliant lecture, said, "Read everything." And I say the same to you—Read everything. Read science? Yes. Read theology? Do not flatter yourself that you are an all-round scientist, even, if you do not. Theology is the queen of the sciences. The intellectual discipline it affords you, if you read it aright, is superior to that of mathematics. Poetry? Of course. The language of man's nobler instincts, the speech of love, the expression of man's passion for God and immortality. Those never find voice for all that is in them but in poetry. Fiction? A little, but not much. The librarian of one of the most famous London libraries spoke the other day of two young lady subscribers who took out of that library eighteen volumes of fiction weekly. A three-volume novel every day of the week! A sure method of committing intellectual suicide, of sinking into a perfumed sea of mud.

The zoologist will show you an animal which once possessed limbs which he has now lost. You have just a small remnant of the limb left, some small sign that the limb was once there. The animal had ceased to use the limbs, its conditions of life had got to be such that it had no need for the limbs, and they dropped off. Cells in the brain that cease to be used dry up, practically become extinct. I have seen a picture intended to be a caricature of what man will get to be if we go on without a break, shouting, "Education, education, intellectual drill,—that is what man needs." Man is represented as a poor, wizened, shrunken creature in everything but the head. The head is huge.

He has got to be all head; a mere calculating machine; a phenomenal brain, and nothing but a brain. Everything else has dropped from him. That would be no more beautiful to me than if he sank back again to be an ape. To be a *man*—that is what you want to be; and if you want to be a man, every faculty in you must be alive. The highest window of the house may be in heaven, but the foundations of the house are in the earth. You must have light for the loftier thing in you that revels in science, and the still loftier thing in you that calls for God. But you must have light for the lower windows also; for the spirit of romance and fancy, of mirth and laughter; for the soul when it is well at ease, as well as when it is wrestling with the darkest problems. Your reading should sweep the whole gamut of your soul, and rouse every faculty in you to its fullest and most vigorous life.

This would not be complete without my adding another word.

2. Books that will specially act upon and stimulate what is best in you, that will build you up in moral health and robustness. *Pâté de fois gras* is poor food. Tell me that you like it, and I will tell you that you are not a healthy man. Zola's novels—and there are English novels that are quite as demoralizing—are grand palaces built of sewer mud. Burn you the bricks in whatever furnace you may, grant if you like that the man is the most gifted genius in Europe, the bricks are mud still, pestilential still. *Tit-Bits!* Well, I acknowledge that *Tit-Bits* is pure, perfectly pure; but you might as well fit yourself for climbing the Alps by making your breakfast of *bonbons*, as fit yourself for understanding any serious problem by reading this last specimen of "milk for babes."

I am half tempted to give you a course of reading, to map out a course of study for you, but I dare not venture. One thing, however, I must do. I must remind you of the rich inheritance which is yours in the noble fields of English literature; the richest, purest, healthiest literature in Europe. One of the things I am proudest of when I begin to think of England is not its navy, nor its commerce, nor its vast colonial posessions, but its literature. The great names in English history to me are—not to mention theologian, or historian, or philosopher—Shakespeare and Milton, Spenser and Cowper, Wordsworth, Tennyson, and Robert Browning. England may some day become a second-rate power, but the nation which numbers those among her sons can never be despised; the man who has access to those sons of genius may spend every leisure hour with the gods. Soak your souls in these. And, above all, *this Book*—the Bible. I speak of it now merely as literature—its grand ideas so nobly and perfectly expressed, its literary beauties, its countless lyrics, its idyls, its one grand drama, its exquisite prayers, its liturgies, its hymns. Young friends, do any of you grieve that you are not better educated? Do you envy those who have enjoyed brilliant advantages denied to you? Envy no one overmuch. The man who has mastered the English Bible has tasted culture in its most perfect form, has mastered the superbest literature the world has ever seen.

III. Once more: How SHALL I READ? What rules must I observe? Please understand, I have nothing to say as to the best methods of reading a book, if you merely wish to reproduce it, to stand an examination in it, or to shine in brilliant talk about it. I am referring rather to the moral uses of a book, to the spirit in which you must pursue all your reading. How shall you read so as to make your reading contribute to your mental and spiritual health, enrich and sweeten your life?

1. See that you digest all you read. We talk sarcastically of the gourmand—the man who believes in eating for its own sake; to whom the cook is the supreme artist, and the only man to whom he pays real deference. His ill health is a mystery to him; he moans over the inscrutable providence that tortures him; but, if he would only see it, there is no mystery in the misery which he suffers. The remedy is an easy one; let him eat less and digest what he eats. We know other gourmands. We know the sermon-gourmand—the man who is never so happy as when he is listening to the famous preachers of the hour, except when he is dilating upon the wonderful sermons he has heard on memorable past occasions. But there is no power of service in him; he has converted no sermon he has ever heard into food; he is a spiritual invalid, often a spiritual dyspeptic, and at best his life evaporates in talk. Then there is the book-gourmand. George Eliot has given us a memorable illustration of him —the man who had spent a long life in reading and taking notes, preparing material for a great work which was to startle the world by-and-by. The great work never appeared, and the man's immense reading remained a mass of undigested ideas, which gradually choked the soul with which God had started him. Books did not help, invigorate, inspire him; they simply smothered him. Oh, I am never afraid of the man of many books, of the man whose boast is his great library. The redoubtable man is the man of few books; the man like the famous Methodist minister who had spent his life with three—Emerson, Shakespeare, and the Bible. His mind teemed with ideas; pearls dropped from him in

the commonest talk. His few books, well digested, meant mental robustness and spiritual health. He never was somebody else, but the noble original self which God had made him, for every idea was well digested.

I have happy memories of the great men of my boyhood, and greatest of all to me were the preachers. The memorable occasions to me were the great religious festivals, when the fathers, the prophets and kings of the Church, honoured and revered, the "masters of assemblies," appeared. I have the vividest recollections of the sermons of those days; they cut lines into my soul which will never be erased; substantial, solid, well grounded in a firm theological basis. The preacher, however much of a poet he might be, never allowed himself to rise on the wings of fancy and imagination until he had first of all laid down a clear, solid statement of the truth or doctrine enunciated in his text. Oh, great master-preachers, ye have left none of your like behind you! Their books were very, very few—they could have carried their libraries with them on their preaching journeys; but the books they had they *knew*. Their books were dissolved like iron in their blood. Men of mental pith and fibre, their mark is upon the Churches to this day; their memory is a romance. Quivering with poetry, daring in their imagination, they always started with solid thinking; always robust, because their mental food was well digested.

2. Convert your reading into work. You *know* nothing until you *do* it. This is especially true of your reading of the Bible. You can only understand the gospel by working out the gospel. "If any man will do His will, he shall know of the doctrine." You understand no doctrine until you have embodied it in life, work, service. You can never

learn botany from books only—learn it so that you can say you know it. You must search among the hedges, and dissect with your knife the flowers which your book describes. When you take to teach your boy chemistry, you do not set him learning long lists of chemical formulæ, which mean no more to him than a page out of a Chinese poem would. Oh, you use the book, of course; but you take him to the laboratory, you set him to verify over his crucibles every statement in the book. If you say that of science, how much more is it true of the Bible! You read it; you master its doctrines, so you think; you pronounce confident opinions upon its claims to determine what you ought to believe. My dear friend, you know nothing about it yet. Take it to the Sunday school; front the haggard conditions that surround our missions with it; see how it will apply to the man who is struggling for a foothold for his faith and finding it hard to believe; sit down with the dying, and see how it answers there. You must work the book into the tissue of your life, use it to solve the stern problems with which life is full. You must take it to the laboratory.

If you do not, I doubt the good which any reading, even the reading of the Bible, can do you. You may demoralize and pauperize your soul even with the Bible, use it as a mere emotional luxury and relax your moral fibre. You are no better, no stronger, no more of a man, because you have merely *read* even the Bible. We acknowledge this with regard to other books. The curse of many is their overmuch reading—reading that expresses itself in no brave service or noble work. The novel-reader who weeps himself blind over the sorrows of his hero, or rocks himself in the tempest through which that hero is struggling into light and victory, and feels himself an angel of mercy, and brave thoughts rush like a breeze through his soul, but whose life breaks into help for no needy fellow-mortal, is fast becoming an abject spiritual pauper. And the man who pours out emotional talk over the Bible, but translates it into no noble service, who weeps plenty but no tear ever crystallizes into any form of Christian work, will eventually be the completest spiritual bankrupt. Reading—even reading the Bible—may be a spiritual snare as well as a help.

3. Bring all your reading to God. I saw a graphic description in a newly published book of the studio of the great French painter who is just now, so the book says, the king of European painting. Every one covets admission into that studio, especially every young painter. To show his work to the master-painter, to have the master give his suggestions, perhaps a word of commendation, sends the young painter back to his work with fresh zest and keener determination. So every earnest-minded reader will constantly bring his reading to God, will pray over every course of reading he proposes to himself. Faraday constantly prayed over his scientific researches. It was no wonder that the laboratory often became a Shechinah to him. I have even seen an edition of Euclid with a prayer on its first page. The geometrician who edited that edition understood that God was the supreme Geometrician, and that the light to understand geometry as well as to expound the Bible must come from Him. I have seen the scientific inquirer bend over his microscope. He sets the instrument in perfect order first, and then well fixes the object he wishes to examine under his glass, and last of all turns a strong light upon the object. That is what I would always do if I were you. Not only when

I read the Bible, but whatever I was reading—theology, or science, or philosophy, or a disquisition on art, or a superb poem—I would turn on the light of God upon it, the light of Him from whom every truth cometh; that is, I would pray.

BLITHE CHILDHOOD AND BLITHER OLD AGE.

BLITHE CHILDHOOD AND BLITHER OLD AGE.

"Thou makest the outgoings of the morning and evening to rejoice."—Ps. lxv. 8.

MORNING, with hope in its eyes and a song on its lips, has lost none of the charms which made poets of men in the days when they could leave their beds to greet it. Fashion, hard work, and the artificial life we live have made us strangers to the morning; morning has disappeared before we see the face of heaven or earth. But there are lines in the faces of both which no one sees but the man who will seek them before the noise of work and the fever of anxiety have begun. A voice of rejoicing greets the dawn which later hours hush. And when the heat and hurry of the day are over, and the invisible hands of earth's guardian angel begin to gather the curtains of evening about her again, a deep restful joy, a spell of perfect peace, falls upon everything. Morning is beautiful; evening, when some moods are upon you, more beautiful. "Thou makest the outgoings of the morning and evening to rejoice."

That is the natural fact, that is the figure, and that typifies another fact. The blithest souls in the world are the children, the youths and maidens from whom the dew of the morning has not yet vanished; and the elders, the grave and grey-headed upon whom the calm and quiet of evening have fallen. You in the rush and turmoil of work, excited, feverish, anxious—you do not taste life's purest, sweetest, and most perfect joys. "Thou makest the out-goings of the *morning* and *evening* to rejoice."

Remain with this for a little while.

I. LIFE BOTH IN PROSPECT AND RETROSPECT IS BEAUTIFUL. To look on at the start, to look back at the close, are both a delight. Old age corroborates childhood, evening renews the morning; and whoever fails to enjoy life, both these succeed, especially under the conditions which I will mention in a moment. Life beats neither the child nor the old man. The start glows with charm, and the end will melt into a still deeper charm.

Now, to the majority of us, to *all* of us who belong to the mid-region of life, life is severe, exacting, even grim; means hard work and the sternest facts. *Business*, if I am to judge from your faces as I see you start to London in the morning, is no byplay. There is no field of battle which a man may not dare, who can face business daily and keep his head clear and his heart pure. It is no wonder to me that men's faces grow hard, suspicious, sour, sad. Martyrs who submitted to be burnt, and who died with all the *éclat* of heroes about them, showed no heroism to be compared with that of the man who can plunge into the competition of city life and still have the courage to read the Sermon on the Mount when he comes home. It is no wonder to me that the poetry and romance die in men; it is half a miracle that the hearts of some of you still bubble fresh and limpid, that your soul carries the music of a mountain-well in it. *Politics* are worse than business. They sour and embitter men, make them hard and cynical. I read the newspapers and wonder that the speeches of many do not blister the tongues that utter them. You never know how you can hate a man, or to what vulgar speech you can condescend, until you sell yourself to politics. The respectable, educated Englishman never becomes a man to shun in the street, never becomes a traitor, until he differs from you in politics. A man shirks his duty who shuns politics, who contributes nothing, not even the weight of his vote, to the discussion of the great questions upon which the well-being of his country depends; but he sets himself a hard task who determines that it shall not poison his spirit or foul his conscience. *Theology*, with its hosts of problems, is a graver matter still. I do not at all wonder that this present generation has almost made up its mind that it will not tolerate theology even in a preacher; that almost everybody wants to convert religion into morality and philanthropy, into teetotalism and careful observance of the laws of health. I saw at one of the public exhibitions the other day a diver shod with iron-laden boots, and with a fantastically devised covering over his head. He was there to exhibit what diving meant; but he looked intensely uncomfortable, and seemed to apologize for his grotesque appearance. And I have often thought that in our foolish preacher's garb I and every brother-minister must often look as ridiculous as he. Preaching is a diving performance, and many will have it that with all our diving we bring up nothing but sham pearls. Many will have it that theology has not one sure, solid truth to give us, that on the great questions which are the basis of religious faith we know nothing. Ah, sometimes preaching is weary work! You spend your life sending down the plummet into the abyss and you can touch no bottom. To be sure, you escape from these despairing moods; befogged for a moment, you get to see clearly again; but even when despair chokes you, you have to pursue your stern task. Business, politics, preaching, are trying tests, but you cannot shirk them; to do so is to fail in duty, to cease to be a *man*.

I am fresh from the reading of Laurence Oliphant's life. Laurence Oliphant, perhaps you say, was a fanatic; his fanaticism had unhinged his mind; he exaggerated the duty of self-abnegation; life for him meant to wash out his own soul to put colour into the life of others. But that is only an exaggeration. To live *is* to serve others. I make no apology when I say I want your money, your best thinking, your hardest work, and the burden of your tasks is sometimes heavy. It was Paul, who never wanted life to be made easy for him, who cried, "I groan, being burdened." And the majority of us are just there to-day; the burden of life's work, cares, anxieties, its crucial questions, is upon us. It is of us that the world demands an answer to its crowded problems—theological, social, questions of Church and creed and the rights of labour—and it is no wonder that sometimes life looks grave, severe, stern, that there is no power in us sometimes to rejoice. Driven, we have no time to be happy, no time sometimes so much as to wipe our brow.

Now, I acknowledge all that. But will you set against it two things?

1. First, the glorious days of childhood, the sweet hours of early life. We often speak of youth's power of prophecy, of the young soul's anticipation of the future, the expectation of what life is going to be; oh, enchanting first days!

BLITHE CHILDHOOD AND BLITHER OLD AGE. 191

But that is not what I mean. I speak of a time that comes before even that—of youth's pure enjoyment of life. "Thou makest the outgoings of the morning . . . to rejoice."

You hang up the Æolian harp in the hedge, and if there be the faintest breath of air it will awake into music. The whole neighbourhood the last ten days has been one mass of blossom. Your gardens have been glorious as Eden; I have seen trees upon which the angels might have dropped their robes in passing. Spring has proved that it has lost none of its ancient charm, that it can still wipe every wrinkle out of the face of the earth with its first touch. The trees have believed in Spring, and poured out their wealth of life in blossom as if proud of their beauty. And so you brave young souls! You believe in life; you open out your souls trustfully to it; you have not begun yet to be suspicious; you do not imagine every cup which life sets to your lips to be poisoned; you *dare* smell every fragrant flower; you believe in to-day as well as yesterday, and you are not afraid of to-morrow with any fresh truth which it may bring. You never feel inclined to suspect every new prophet to be a traitor, and every new book to have the inspiration of the evil one in it. You are willing to hear every new call that comes; the charm has not disappeared for you from the work of the Lord, and you could know no shame so great as to be dismissed from His service. No prophecy has ever failed to you—"the Word of the Lord standeth sure;" you discount nothing which God has promised, and the fulfilment will be richer than the promise itself. Welcome, life! Hail, blessed future! "The outgoings of the morning . . . rejoice."

2. The retrospect will be blither still. Believe me, the brightest season is yet to be. "And the *evening* to rejoice."

The surging process through which your faith may be passing will be over, and your faith will be richer than ever. The scares which many of us have through criticism; through the testing fires into which the Word of God is cast; through the rapid succession of books that come questioning the authority of the Bible, absolutely denying its right to the deference it has always received; through the breaking up of old forms of thought, the recasting of old theories, the new terms in which we have got to speak of the Atonement and future retribution;—this scare will have ceased. The confusion and uncertainty in which you feel as if everything were breaking up and you were losing every truth you had treasured most, will have passed into a firm hold of all absolute verities.

I spent a day not long since in a famous foundry. I watched the whole process by which the superbest machinery was constructed; saw the design ingeniously cut out in sand—the very figure the designer had in his mind cut out as clearly as these notes of mine are written on the page before me—and by-and-by the whole sand-heap bricked and buttressed about until to my unpractised eye it all looked a meaningless mass of confusion. But the design which the master-mind was aiming at was all the while there, and presently I saw it, so exquisite in its lines and sweep, produced in solid metal. So—shall I put it in the first person?—I remember when every truth in this gospel to me was broken up into utter confusion; everything seemed to have disappeared in a cloud of books and criticisms and new theories. I could not descry one clear line. But I have come out into a sure faith—God, love, an atonement which is a glory to God and a joy to me, a hope so universal that I say sometimes that God will not fail to bring one soul home; in any case, that love will win a triumph which will make God the absolute Victor. God is not going to be baffled. My evening is never more going to be disturbed; henceforth life is going to be absolutely calm. "Thou makest the outgoings of the ... *evening* to rejoice."

II. THE PROSPECT AND THE RETROSPECT ARE BOTH MADE BEAUTIFUL BY GOD. Youth and old age—it is God touches both into beauty. Not one word of what I have said is true apart from God. Youth possesses no power of joy but in Him, old age is ugly severed from Him; the morning opens with the mutterings of a storm, evening closes in blackness and hopelessness. God puts into both the lines that constitute their charm.

1. Youth and old age specially need God—need God as none others do. I once saw Titian's most famous picture of the "Assumption of the Virgin" in the art-gallery at Venice. The tradition is that Titian merely designed the picture, drew outlines of the figures—of Mary and those who saw heaven open to receive her. Others, ordinary painters, could fill in the outlines; and when that was done, Titian came again and gave the picture its few last touches. He designed it—began the painting of it—and he completed it.

So exactly here. It is the first modelling of life, the giving to life its first form, which is important. It is that you give your children's souls the first bent; it is the dread of putting a dent into them which will mean desperate cost for them to get rid of by-and-by that staggers you, and makes you half afraid of life. Young people, you know how dear you are to me. I pray for you, I dream of you, but you sometimes make me half afraid to come here to preach. You love me and believe in me, and I tremble when I remember that the conception of God *I* give you is what you believe in, that you will determine your relations to Christian service according to what you hear from me. I wonder whether some of you will refrain from committing yourselves to that service because of what you hear me say; whether you will ever wish that you had never heard me; whether I shall help to *make* or *mar* you. But I will tell you the one thing that gives me confidence. I know the God who can set life on the right lines for you; who can make you strong, wise, brave; who can save you from the mistakes which end in disaster, and lead to endless sorrow; and whatever else I may forget, I will never forget to bring you to Him. I will preach to you the love of God, the Fatherhood of God, the Cross—the anthem of the divine compassion—and the heaven of God shall always shine like a beacon before you. I will not lead you to the bleak uplands of the Fall and the first sin—we may sometimes have to get there, but not often; not through the sandy deserts of doctrines which neither you nor I can understand; you will not hear overmuch of the terrors of hell, nor the "fearful looking for of judgment and fiery indignation," from me. I will take you through the sweet valleys of the divine love and help and hope. You shall walk with God in perfect confidence. The grace of God shall at least draw the first lines of the picture. Life shall begin there; the "outgoings of the morning" shall "rejoice."

And, fathers and mothers—God alone can complete the picture; touch you into the beauty that will perfect the work of life. You are brave and calm; you have passed through the strain of work; you have fought many a sturdy battle for the faith, for truth, for purity. Some of us think sometimes that life can do no more for you; that God leaves you here simply that we may see into what beauty it is possible for man to grow, even upon earth. But one touch or more may still be necessary, and your old age shall end in perfect gladness. "Thou makest the outgoings of the . . . evening to rejoice."

2. To early life and old age God is an actual and beautiful fact. I have seen three generations living under the same roof—the old man whose work is over; the son, the real head of the household; and the merry-hearted children—the boys and girls who are beginning to open their eyes in wonder at the wealth and glory of the world in which they find themselves placed. The gravest face there is that of the strong man in the prime of life, who is in the thick of work, confronted by life's numberless problems. He has many mental struggles, and has found no complete or consistent theory of life yet. Oh, he believes in God, and has some hope that some day he will be able to see the love and wisdom which gird it; but in the mean while its sorrows and sufferings, its many mysteries, wound him. If he be a poet, he breaks out now and then in dirges and lamentations, sometimes in daring defiances of the fate that determines all things. If he be a philosopher, he calls himself a pessimist, and the shadow of his pessimism is in his face. Not so the boy. The wealth of life is a wonder to him; God is everywhere, and to be alive is an ecstasy. And for the old man, the doubts, the misgivings, the scepticisms that killed his courage, are over. The tree which moaned and sighed in the wintry winds is cut down. The cunning man gets hold of it, and out of its wood fashions the violin—sensitive as his own soul. The musician draws his bow across it; sweet memories of the

wood are in it; it awakes at his touch, and it sobs and sighs; the wail of the winds is in it still. But this is only a prelude. The instrument that can tell that is just the instrument to tell also the most perfect ecstasy, and the song which was a moan at first ends in a burst of victory. That violin is the soul of man. The man who has been most sorely tried is always the man who sings the clearest song of perfect trust; life becomes a triumph to you as you listen to him; the sorrows through which you have passed lift your faith to its most triumphant notes.

You have climbed through a narrow mountain-pass. Morning was radiant when you started, and every foot you climbed the scene became more enchanting, and your spirits rose with every step. But presently the prospect narrows, the mountains close in upon you, the sun is hidden, and a cold wind sweeps through the defile; your spirits droop, and you can only doggedly plod along. But by-and-by the mountains open out again, the pass is over, and far away under your feet stretches a fairer scene than that which thrilled you in the early morning. Many of you, perhaps, are to-day in the pass. Youth is a memory which you find it hard to realize; you have left it far behind you. But you will be out of the pass soon. The prospect will open out again, and the sun will set upon a fairer world than you have ever seen. The best of life is yet to come. "Thou makest the outgoings of the *morning* and *evening* to rejoice."

III. AND NOW WE CHEER OURSELVES AMID THE TASKS AND DISCIPLINES OF MID-LIFE WITH THOUGHTS OF BOTH. I will think of the morning and of the evening also.

1. I will remember the enchanting days of early morning. This is not so easy, perhaps, as you imagine, and

I feel indebted to every one who can help me to do it. A delightful new literature has appeared within the last few years—a children's literature. Its one salient feature is this—that those who have given us its most fascinating specimens have the genius to remember what they were when they were children. Oh, I have read them; they have given me back my early youth; I have become a boy again; I have rediscovered my childhood, my absolute delight in life, and the radiant morning when as yet I did not know what it was to be afraid of God.

> "There is a scent upon the brier,
> A tremulous splendour in the autumn dews,
>   Cold morns are fringed with fire;
> Daisies are white upon the churchyard sod,
>   Sweet tears the clouds bear down and give.
> This world is very lovely; O my God,
>   I thank Thee that I live"—

sang the young poet, and I was a poet then. Heaven was about us in our infancy, and the chill breath of doubt had blasted none of its beauty. Jesus was the welcome Interpreter of life, and no word of His had become a yoke to me yet. Happy early days! ye have engraved yourselves on my heart, and I mean to carry you with me for ever.

2. I will often sit down with the elders, with those who are fathers indeed; who, however old they become, never cease to be young; who, upon the verge of the grave, keep themselves immersed in the work and hopes of the present hour; who always read the last book, and keep themselves in touch with the last new idea. The youngest man I know has long since passed ninety. The questions he always asks are about the young, about their way of stating the problems which confronted him more than seventy years

ago. He never rebukes and anathematizes them because their theories are often crude and their judgments over-hasty. The crude theories are only the preliminary to careful and reverent thinking. Oh, he can listen, suggest, guide; his is the youngest heart I know.

Some years ago I stood in a northern port watching the whale-fishers sailing out to the northern seas. Some were going out for the first time, with strong work in their sinews, and the flash of excitement in their faces. But the old men were there also. There was no going out to the northern seas again for them—they had made their last voyage; but they were there to wish good fortune to the younger men, their sons and grandsons. And when the vessels put out to sea, they waved their blessing after them. So the fathers always do. You, young people, are going out to the work of life, to the great tasks of the hour. There are stirring times before you, hard work, tasks that will test your faith and courage. But you are men of mettle; you will, I know, be strong. The fathers believe in you, and have handed over their tasks to you. They bid you God-speed, set their hands upon your heads and bless you. See to it that in the summing up of all things you have a good record.

3. And when evening comes for me I will quietly, hopefully, and confidently wait. And the significance and beauty of life will grow upon me as I wait. The disciplines which have hurt me most, providences against which I most bitterly protested, will grow into most signal proofs of the love that has ordered all, and the end shall be perfect peace.

I was staying a while ago on the broad estuary of one of our noblest Welsh rivers. When I looked out through my window the first thing in the morning, I could clearly see the land on the other side. When the day became hot, a haze filled the atmosphere, and I looked in vain for it. But when the cool of evening came, and I looked again, the shore yonder was clearly visible once more, and I could count the fields and the homesteads. And so, when I was a child, heaven was clear to me—as sure as the fields in which I played. Often since have I lost it, and declared in black unbelief that the dream of heaven was a delusion. But evening is coming, and I see it again.

> "Sweet fields, beyond the swelling flood,
> Stand dressed in living green."

My last doubt has disappeared. "Thou makest the outgoings . . . of the evening to rejoice."

CONSIDERATENESS.

CONSIDERATENESS.

"Let your considerateness be known unto all men."—PHIL. iv. 5.

I WANT to get away as far as possible this morning from the great subjects, the awful subjects, that I have been talking about lately. I want a break. You can dwell too long in the same neighbourhood. Even the gospel, in its sublime subjects—the Cross, the Atonement, Faith, the choice which determines your destiny—and those are the subjects that I have been talking about for weeks now without a break—may become half-oppressive. It cows you. This morning I will talk of one of the moralities—one of the "minor moralities," as Edward White calls them—one of the Christian moralities, of course. I am not sure that Moses had it in his mind among the stern moralities which he cut into the list of our duties to one's neighbour. I dare say I could fit it in somewhere if I tried. But in any case it is one of the Christian moralities. Be considerate; "let your considerateness be known unto all men."

Many men are orthodox, self-denying, great in sacrifice; the stuff out of which martyrs are made is in them; they blaze into enthusiasms, they spend themselves in grand enterprises, but they are harsh and over-exacting in their judgments; they never imagine that any one needs pity;

they drive roughshod over the sensitivenesses of men, and their softest word is a whip. To be sure, they are Christians —full of strength, force, and energy; always flaming with zeal that never wearies, never complains; the backbone of the Church. But they are not Christians of the noblest type, certainly not of the loveliest type; lacking still the last grace that makes a man perfect. "Considerateness" I have called it. "Moderation" you have it in the Old Version. But that scarcely gives the specific idea in the Greek word. "Forbearance" the Revised Version makes it; "gentleness" you have it in the margin. But this word gives it exactly—"*considerateness.*" "Let your considerateness be known unto all men."

I. AND NOW, TO START WITH, THE CHRISTIAN CONCEPTION OF LIFE INCLUDES THE SMALLEST VIRTUES. It never says of any virtue, however insignificant, "Oh, this is of no importance; a man may be without this and be none the worse for it." Observe—

1. The grandest virtues are often smeared, and so marred, by some small vice. A man's gifts are often so rare, he is a man of such unmistakable genius, he possesses such signal powers of service, that we ignore his vices. The statesman who has no rival, who is evidently born to rule, of whom every one thinks, to whom every one instinctively turns in every grave crisis—history is full of illustrations—is often bemired with immorality, and there is a tacit understanding between everybody never to mention that. There have been poets who have so intoxicated the world with their music that every one is not only too ready to make apologies for their vices, but to talk as if the vice which would damn the ordinary man were some half-virtue in the man of genius—the hall-mark, the best proof that he *is* a

man of genius. Art, we say, in the poet or painter is independent of morality, and to talk of the immorality of Burns or Shelley is simply to prove that we are poor cramped souls to whom it would be impossible to explain what art means. Opium-eating, to be sure, is an offensive vice in a Chinee, but it is half-interesting in De Quincey or Coleridge : it would have been almost a pity that De Quincey should not have tried opium-eating ; we should have lost one of the most enchanting chapters in English literature. And so also when we come to still smaller vices. We half like the everlasting snarl that was upon Carlyle's face. The man's gifts bewitch us, and when we can find no excuse for it, we get to half doubt whether a man can be a man of genius unless there be a scar upon his face ; we are not sure that we should like him without the scar.

Let us come back to first principles again. A vice is a vice wherever it is found, and an uglier vice in the man who is clothed in rare gifts. A hare-lip is all the uglier because it is on an otherwise beautiful face; and a sour temper, a sulky mood, a jealous disposition which breaks the peace of a household, mars you all the more, because God has endowed you with gifts which He intended to be like martial music to others. Every one who knows you should be braver, blither, more clear-headed, and better fitted for work. What intent had God, think you, in clothing you with such gifts, if it was not for this ? I may excuse petty vices in some small soul ; but you, gifted child of God—I cannot excuse them in you.

Some one was showing me the other day a grand vase, a bit of genuine art-work, which he had in his drawing-room. Nobody could fail to notice it, and I had seen it the moment I entered the room. "But look here," said the owner, and he turned the vase round; "it is this that spoils it." And I looked closer, and there was the slightest possible flaw in it. "It is this that condemns it," said the owner. And it did condemn it; and somehow, whenever I see the upon-the-whole exquisite work of art, it is that flaw that I always think of first. Whether it be turned towards me or not, I always *see* it; I can never forget that it is there. So the strong, gifted soul, brilliant with many virtues—if there be one flaw in him, I may forget his virtues, but I can never, somehow, forget the flaw. I may never take the trouble to look at the sun; but now and then, when its black spots are specially visible, I am sure to take the telescope and get a good long look at *them*, and assure myself how pronounced and unmistakable they are. The weakness, the infirmity, the *flaw*, never escapes me; some ugly spirit in me compels me to see that.

2. Again: The superbest capacities, the most radiant gifts, may be nullified by some small, mean vice. Clog one note in the organ behind me, and it will defy the most accomplished musician that can sit down to it; no one can get music out of it. You do not need a terrific storm to wreck your ship. The stateliest ship that was ever built, you have only to allow one leak in it, and it may sink in perfect calm. So the most gifted soul; the most brilliant writer, or the painter whose first picture every one hailed—a fresh soul had appeared, who had discovered a new light in the face of nature, and he was to herald in a new era in art—success dimmed his eyes, robbed his fingers of their delicate touch; luxury which money brought choked his soul, and he has become dull and fashionable, and can teach the world nothing. The business man—I have been here long enough to see the beginning and the end of scores—

who stood on the threshold of life five and twenty years ago; London was at the young man's feet; every one prophesied a brilliant career for him; born with every gift, clothed in the very graces which command confidence and win in business. But he failed—not abjectly, but he failed—and his failure has been a wonder to many. Petty vices which you would not dignify by calling them sins; a glass of sherry at eleven o'clock, and the persuasion that one of his missions in life was to see that England reared a breed of race-horses which the world could not surpass, have kept him to this day, with all his unquestioned genius, almost at the bottom of the ladder. I am not sure, young men, that I can tell you how you may inevitably succeed in business and win fortunes; but I can tell you how to fail. A heavy lunch every day, crowned, of course, with ale or wine, and small bets in as many sweepstakes as possible. You need not be a *roué*, or a drunkard, or write false cheques; small, mean vices will wreck you, however superbly gifted you may be.

I feel bound to add another word. Public life is a matter of concern to everybody. It is everybody's concern as to what the public rulers of England, the men who legislate for England, should be. Politics should be a career for which a man should educate himself as carefully as if he were educating himself for medicine, for the pulpit, or the bar. But that is not enough. A man may be a man of the most brilliant gifts; he may have drilled these to a point of almost absolute perfection, prepared and fitted himself for public work, be *ready* to work and ambitious to work. But there are moral decencies that are absolutely incumbent upon the most gifted soul. No man who aspires to a place in the public service of his country must be permitted to outrage these; no nation which is not to blush for itself can ignore these. It may have to banish its most gifted sons in sorrow, but banish them it must. Life is hard and stern; but were it not that it is hard and stern, the world long ago would have been wrecked. There are matters in which the sternest judgment is the most merciful—merciful to the many, and merciful to the sinner as well.

So much for the wrecks of life, the disasters of life, through lack of the minor moralities. And now, secondly—

II. AMONG THE MINOR MORALITIES "CONSIDERATENESS" TAKES A HIGH PLACE. One of the minor virtues urged and emphasized by Paul—" Let your *considerateness* be known unto all men." Considerateness is not indifference. When I say, in your judgment of your neighbour, your comrades in business, the members of your Church, your minister, your children, "be considerate," I do not mean— be indifferent. It is easy enough to be indifferent; easy enough to say it is of no consequence to me what a man is. It is easy enough even to be "just," as we say; though what we call justice is often the grossest injustice. Paul could be severe. Some of the sternest words in the New Testament were spoken by Paul; his words were lashes. I should say that he was a man for whom it had once been specially difficult to be considerate; it was a lesson he had *taught* himself, a virtue into which he had drilled himself. "Let your considerateness be known unto all men." Look at it for a moment.

1. And first: Be not in an over-hurry in forming your judgments of men. There is more wealth, more worth, in most men than you imagine at first sight. Many had passed through the gold-fields of Australia and had never

dreamt of the store of wealth that lay hidden in the uncanny region. It was the dreariest and most uninteresting country in the world, with its monotonous hills in which there was not one picturesque line. Every one hurried through, eager only to get away from this most depressing scenery. But some day a man who had the eye to see passed through. "There is gold in every one of these hills," he said; and in one day the poverty-stricken country became an Eldorado, and everybody hurried to it.

So in other matters. The book in which some rare soul —a man with the lightning in his brain, and the summer shower in his heart—has buried himself;—its first reviewer tosses it on one side with contempt. It is true that he has only half read it; cut a sufficient number of its leaves to get enough material to write his contemptuous review, and to win his fee. It is only by-and-by the man reads it who understands how sacred is the reviewer's work; that to *review* is to taste the new wine, to cut the first road into untravelled territories, to discover the new wealth in quarries that have never been worked. *He* comes, and we find that we have been despising a gold-field. England went mad with laughter over Carlyle's "Sartor Resartus." But there is more gold in that than we have discovered even yet. It was the fashion for many years to make small jokes, to be *smart*, over Robert Browning. We have discovered at last that Browning is a gold-field; we shall spend many years yet before we have discovered all the gold there is in him, the richest mind of the century. Shakespeare, of whom we are so proud to-day, was a stranger to us until Goethe found him. It was Goethe introduced him to Europe, introduced him even to England—showed us what we really possessed in this man of a myriad-sided soul. And the wisest, richest comments on Shakespeare to this day come from the home of Goethe. Do not be in an over-hurry in forming your judgments of men. "Let your considerateness be known unto all men."

Especially—and I have been coming deliberately to this —be not in an over-hurry in passing judgment upon new enterprises, new methods of doing good, new forms of Church work. It is very easy to sum up a new enterprise in the Church with a sneer. You strike out into new lines of thought, new lines in theology, new methods of work, and uncharitable souls, who have never given five minutes' thought to the matter, like a cloud of wasps will sting you into running away from it if they can. The Salvation Army —or perhaps it would be correcter to say, Mr. Booth—is at this moment on his trial. It is easy to say smart things about the Salvation Army. The same smart things were said about John Wesley a hundred years ago. It is easy to shiver when you hear the Salvation Army drum, and to show the ridiculousness of grotesque bonnets and red jerseys. But the man must be worse than blind who weighs the worth of a great religious movement, a new crusade, against bonnets and jerseys. People have got to make all manner of petty charges against Mr. Booth's "Darkest England" scheme. Brilliant leading articles appear in newspapars, and divine criticisms are passed upon the poor prophet and his scheme at fashionable dinner-parties over plentiful champagne. It is so wonderfully good of such people to keep this extravagant enthusiast in his proper place! And this unfashionable impostor has, of course, been working twenty years at his scheme. Oh no, just eighteen months! A pest upon criticism, say I. For very shame, let us be silent. Let us pray for the man, let us lay some small tax upon our luxuries and help the man. But we will cease to criticize for a while, at least; we will give him a few years to show what he may be able to do. "Let your considerateness be known unto all men."

2. Then, do not expect too much. Extravagant expectations are cruel. They show that you fail to realize the conditions under which many have to strive. The schoolmaster who cannot wait for the young mind to unfold, and who cannot be content, for a while at least, with small results, has proved his unfitness to be a teacher. Dr. Arnold never forgot the tearful protest of the dull scholar who looked up into the great man's face and half sobbed, "Why are you angry, sir? I am doing my best." Dr. Arnold had never understood what torture a seemingly easy task may be to a dull boy. But Dr. Arnold was a gentleman as well as a Christian; he begged the lad's pardon; he never forgot the rebuke; and never again failed to be patient with the dullest.

The man is an ungenerous reader of history, and an unjust judge, who expects the young nation which is just beginning to handle the tools of liberty, to exhibit as ripe fruits of civilization as the nation which has grown old in the use of those tools. Liberty is often a dangerous weapon in the hands of an infant nation, but it will soon learn the use of the weapon, and handle it as wisely and deftly as any.

So it is cruel to expect too much from those who are mastering the first lessons of the gospel, who are getting their first foothold in the Christian life. It seems easy to you. You have inherited no vicious taint; it has cost you nothing to believe; your soul has opened as naturally to the gospel as flowers open to the sunshine; there are no stubborn twists, no unholy lusts, in your nature. Wine was never a temptation to you; scepticism never bewitched you for an hour; the way of life has always for you been an easy one. Ah! little do you know how much it costs many to win every yard of the road. You have cut your way up the face of the glacier before now; you dug steps for yourself with your ice-axe, until by-and-by you stood on the mountain summit. To many the Christian life means cutting a way for themselves up the face of the glacier. They only mount foot by foot. Be patient with such; "let your considerateness be known" to such.

If not, I will tell you what the end will be. You will become a cynic, and that is the ugliest type of man. You will become the character depicted in "Robert Elsmere"—the brilliant scholar, the man of culture, who gave up teaching because he could not find any one who was worth trying to teach; who began by despising others, and ended by despising himself, and shrinking with horror at the thought of what he was getting to be—the Nemesis that always overtakes the cynic. You will become another Carlyle, on his weaker side—begin to pelt contemptuous scorn at your brother-man; to imagine it is great to coin bitter phrases, and cheer the world by reminding it that its children are "mostly fools." You would not land yourself there, would you? Nay, we will remember that man is weak and ignorant and often weary; we will believe that, however blunderingly, he is always endeavouring to lift himself a little higher, and we will endeavour to serve him, "giving patience its perfect work." We will set this commandment ever before us: "Let your considerateness be known unto all men."

III. ATTENTION TO THIS WILL WIN FOR THE GOSPEL

VICTORIES THAT NOTHING ELSE WILL. "Considerateness" will do what argument, what zeal, what passionate crusades and missions, fail to do. "Let your considerateness be known unto all men."

1. Considerateness will break down people's opposition to the gospel. Be patient with men and the gospel will inevitably win them. Pelt a man, and you will arouse the devil in him. Expect too much from men, and you will get nothing; expect people to walk too fast, and they will refuse to walk at all. The snow fortress may be an impregnable fortress; you may pelt it, cannonade it, and you produce no impression upon it. But wait for the spring sunshine, and it will melt and disappear. Argument, scorn, expostulation, are cannon-balls; considerateness is the sunshine. You may *melt* the opposition which defied every direct attack.

Your boy has caught the first fever of scepticism. Attack him. You may as well try to get rid of your child's fever with a whip. Begin to argue with him; prime yourself with books, and when you think you are ready, open an assault upon him when he least expects it. Depend upon it, he will rather like that; perhaps he may prove nimbler in argument than you. Every young enthusiast for swordfencing likes practice. Then, if he beats you, do not fail to lose your temper, look shocked, sting him with covert allusions at the dinner-table, talk about the wickedness of "free-thinking," hint slyly at him in family prayer. And the result will be that you will lose him; you will exasperate and help to damn him. You will drive one more away from Jesus Christ.

Friends, hear me. Do not get into a panic because your boy gets into the fever of scepticism for a while;

unless you irritate the fever by constant meddling, it will do him no more harm than the measles. Do not lose your faith in God because the boy gets a passion for the theatre. Let your bright, brave mother's love, your strong, healthy, hopeful trust still shine upon him. Let the song which hovered over his cradle hover over him still; let your heart's sunshine find him, and his scepticism, his young vagabondage, will melt about his head, and make him blush at the thought that he has ever wounded you. You will *win* him. "Let your considerateness be known unto all men."

2. Be considerate, and you will discover *means* of winning; men always reveal themselves to him who can be considerate. You remember the old fable. The North Wind and the Sun set themselves to see which of them could move the traveller to throw off his cloak. The North Wind said, "I will *compel* him," and it blew its iciest blasts; it whipped the man with its bitterest lashes, and the man shivered and drew his cloak closer round himself. The Sun shone upon the traveller with unclouded face, poured upon him its warmest beams, and very soon the cloak had been discarded. And so here: one man is strong in rebukes; he whips you with reproaches, lashes you with reminders of your failures, shows you how feeble you have been, how miserably you have broken down, what ugly lines there are in your life. Oh! it is all true, but you can never open yourself out to such a one. He will never heal you, for you will never give him the chance to heal you; you will gather your cloak closer about yourself, and abandon yourself to sullen defiance and silent misery. But another man shines love and sympathy upon you, and his very look says, "I understand; I know how hard the fight has been, and

I pledge myself to help you if I can." And your poor soul opens itself; and you make him your "father confessor." He has won you, and you hide nothing from him.

Now, that alone is victory; to *win* is the only victory. We have shown how weak and unfounded are the objections which sceptic and secularist, positivist and agnostic, make to our faith—at least, we think we have shown it. We have dislodged their guns, and for the moment there is silence all along the line. We have proved—at least, so we think—that the bitter railing of the working classes who, like Homer's Achilles, have withdrawn from the Churches, and, with proud talk of Christian brotherhood, have pitched their tents outside the camp,—we have proved that they have no cause of complaint. But, dear friends, listen: our arguments, our proofs, have been like the North Wind. We have only succeeded in making those whom we have tried to conquer gather their cloaks closer round themselves. That is no victory. Sit down quietly with such and listen to their tale. Let them tell the whole story there is in them. Let them feel that you also have tasted their difficulties, and that in Jesus you have found a solution. You will steal into them before they know it, will win them before they even suspect it. *That* is victory; *that alone* is victory. "Let your considerateness be known unto all men."